Anxiety Workbook
12 weeks

www.gratitudeandmore.ca

Anxiety and panic can be debilitating and have the power to change the very fabric of our lives. The symptoms can range from a fast heartbeat to the inability to leave your home. I have experienced generalized anxiety since I was thirteen and although I haven't had a panic attack for a number of years, I can and still do get anxious, especially when faced with a new situation or confronted with something I'm not sure I can handle. The great news is that I have learned that I **can** handle it, that it won't kill me–and so far my success rate for surviving panic attacks is 100%.

Although every person is different, we all have a list of things that cause us stress (some things would cause anyone stress). But there is also that list that is unique to us. There is no one size fits all solution for anxiety and panic, but my hope is that this journal will become another tool in your toolbox–one that will not only help provide some relief over anxiety but that will also help you recognize your strength and courage.

For more information on the wide variety of journals we offer, visit us at www.gratitudeandmore.ca

Journal—see where it takes you!

Leah

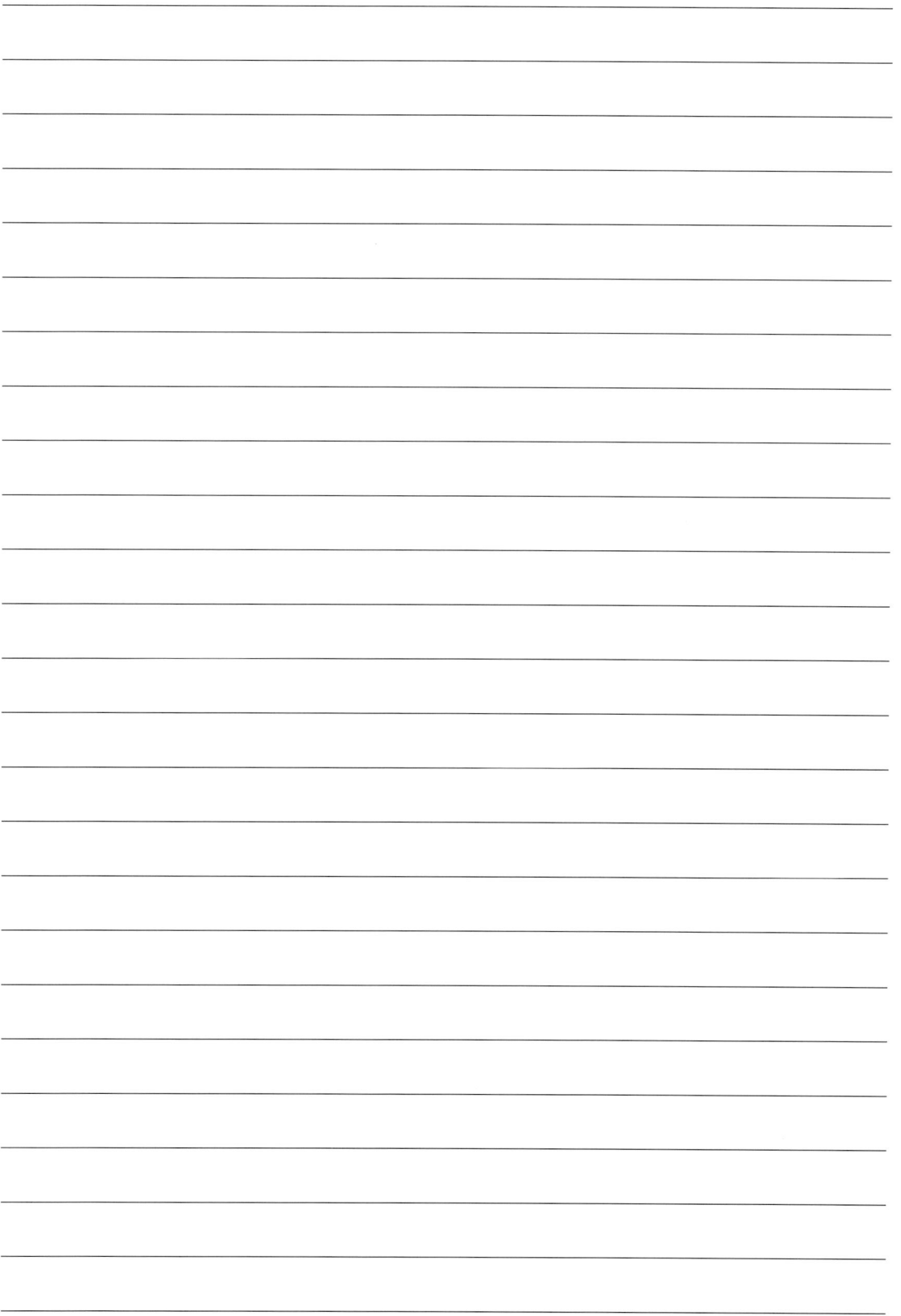

Date:	Anxiety Scale (1-10): AM PM
Today was I compassionate with myself or critical?	Are my thoughts giving me power or taking it away?

Are my thoughts true? *Really true?*

Am I avoiding something that I need to deal with?

Am I forecasting the future?

Am I "catastrophizing"?

Did I experience fear today?	Did it actually come true?
What helps to ease my anxiety?	Did I remember that?
Did I nourish my body and drink enough water?	Did I get fresh air?
How did I move my body today?	Did I try to practice mindfulness and deep breathing?
Did I have "What if's" today?	I am grateful for:

Promise me you'll always remember:
You're braver than you believe, stronger than you seem and smarter than you think.
A.A. Milne

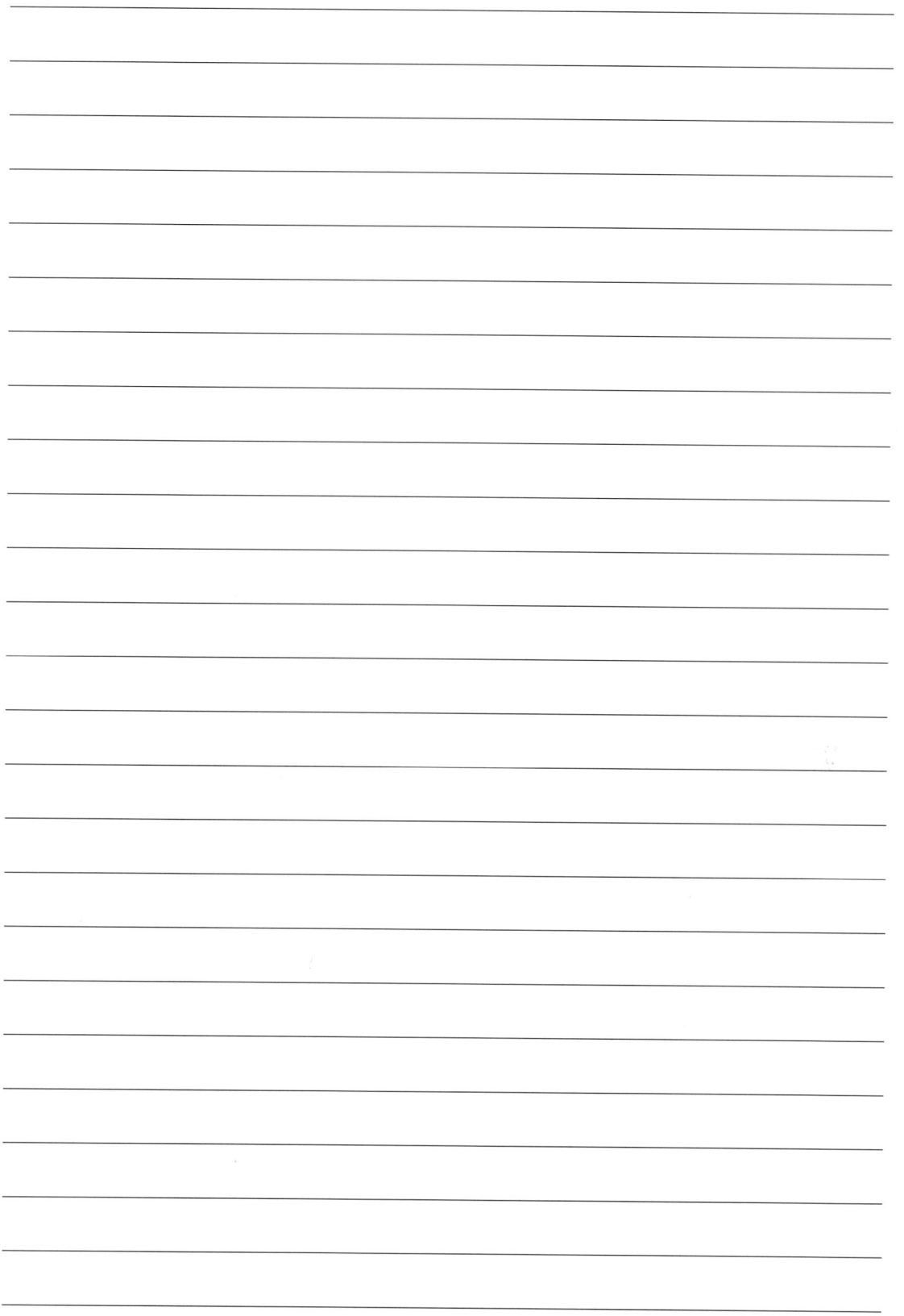

Date:	Anxiety Scale (1-10): AM PM
Today was I compassionate with myself or critical?	Are my thoughts giving me power or taking it away?

Are my thoughts true? *Really true?*

Am I avoiding something that I need to deal with?

Am I forecasting the future?

Am I "catastrophizing"?

Did I experience fear today?	Did it actually come true?
What helps to ease my anxiety?	Did I remember that?
Did I nourish my body and drink enough water?	Did I get fresh air?
How did I move my body today?	Did I try to practice mindfulness and deep breathing?
Did I have "What if's" today?	I am grateful for:

Promise me you'll always remember:
You're braver than you believe, stronger than you seem and smarter than you think.
A.A. Milne

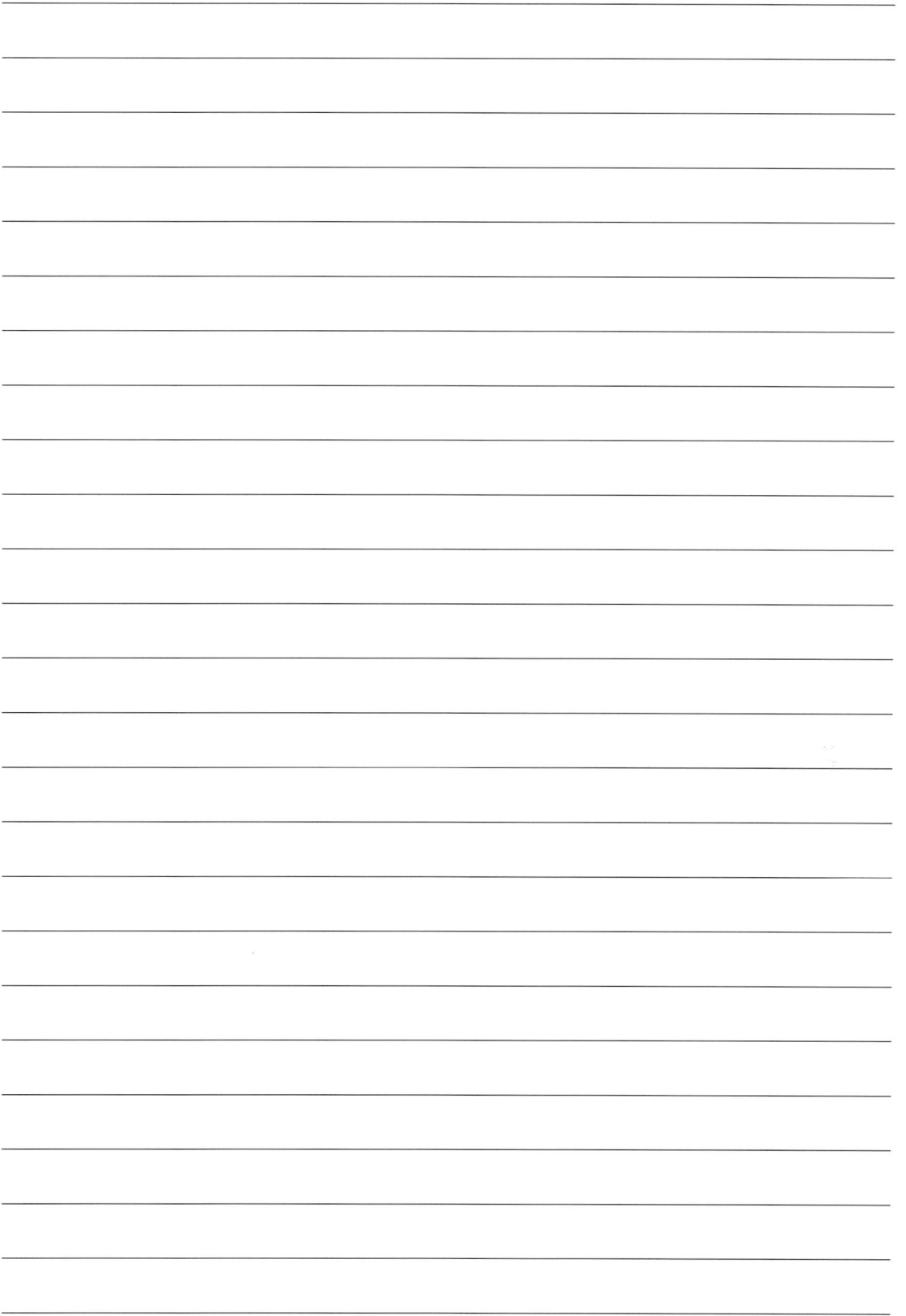

Date:	Anxiety Scale (1-10): AM PM
Today was I compassionate with myself or critical?	Are my thoughts giving me power or taking it away?

Are my thoughts true? *Really true?*

Am I avoiding something that I need to deal with?

Am I forecasting the future?

Am I "catastrophizing"?

Did I experience fear today?	Did it actually come true?
What helps to ease my anxiety?	Did I remember that?
Did I nourish my body and drink enough water?	Did I get fresh air?
How did I move my body today?	Did I try to practice mindfulness and deep breathing?
Did I have "What if's" today?	I am grateful for:

Promise me you'll always remember:
You're braver than you believe, stronger than you seem and smarter than you think.
A.A. Milne

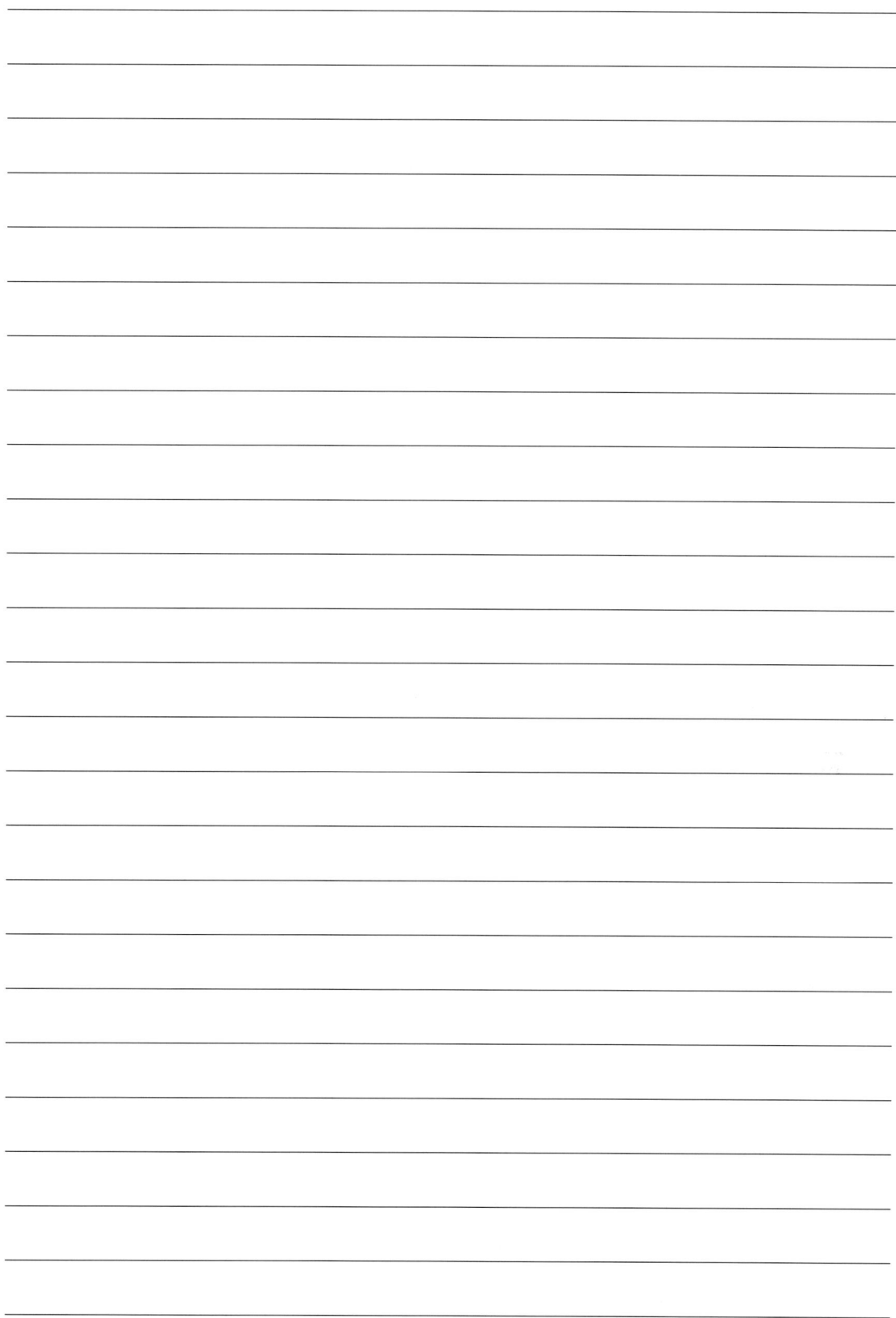

Date:	Anxiety Scale (1-10): AM PM
Today was I compassionate with myself or critical?	Are my thoughts giving me power or taking it away?

Are my thoughts true? *Really true?*

Am I avoiding something that I need to deal with?

Am I forecasting the future?

Am I "catastrophizing"?

Did I experience fear today?	Did it actually come true?
What helps to ease my anxiety?	Did I remember that?
Did I nourish my body and drink enough water?	Did I get fresh air?
How did I move my body today?	Did I try to practice mindfulness and deep breathing?
Did I have "What if's" today?	I am grateful for:

Promise me you'll always remember:
You're braver than you believe, stronger than you seem and smarter than you think.
A.A. Milne

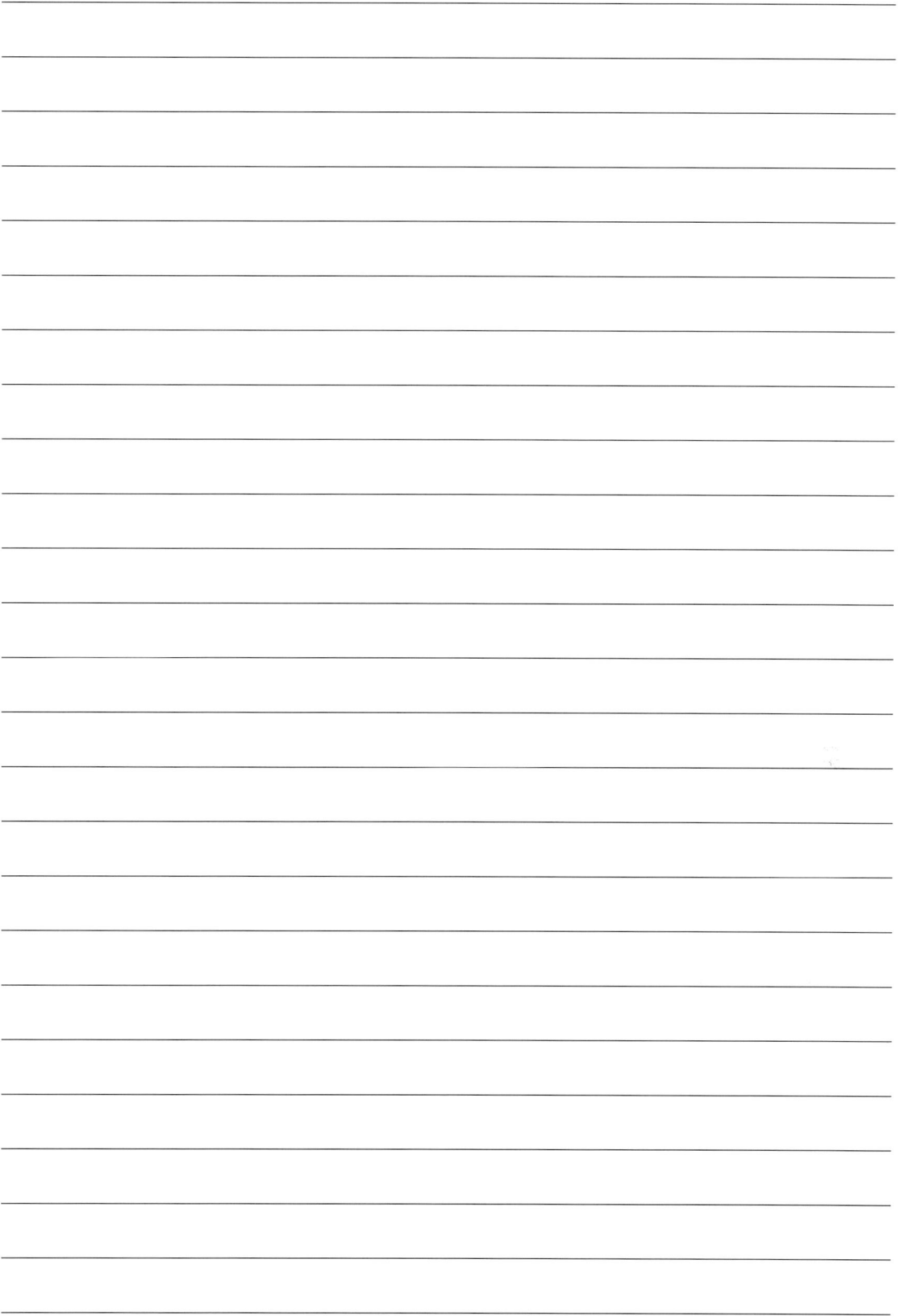

| Date: | Anxiety Scale (1-10): |
	AM PM
Today was I compassionate with myself or critical?	Are my thoughts giving me power or taking it away?

Are my thoughts true? *Really true?*

Am I avoiding something that I need to deal with?

Am I forecasting the future?

Am I "catastrophizing"?

Did I experience fear today?	Did it actually come true?
What helps to ease my anxiety?	Did I remember that?
Did I nourish my body and drink enough water?	Did I get fresh air?
How did I move my body today?	Did I try to practice mindfulness and deep breathing?
Did I have "What if's" today?	I am grateful for:

Promise me you'll always remember:
You're braver than you believe, stronger than you seem and smarter than you think.
A.A. Milne

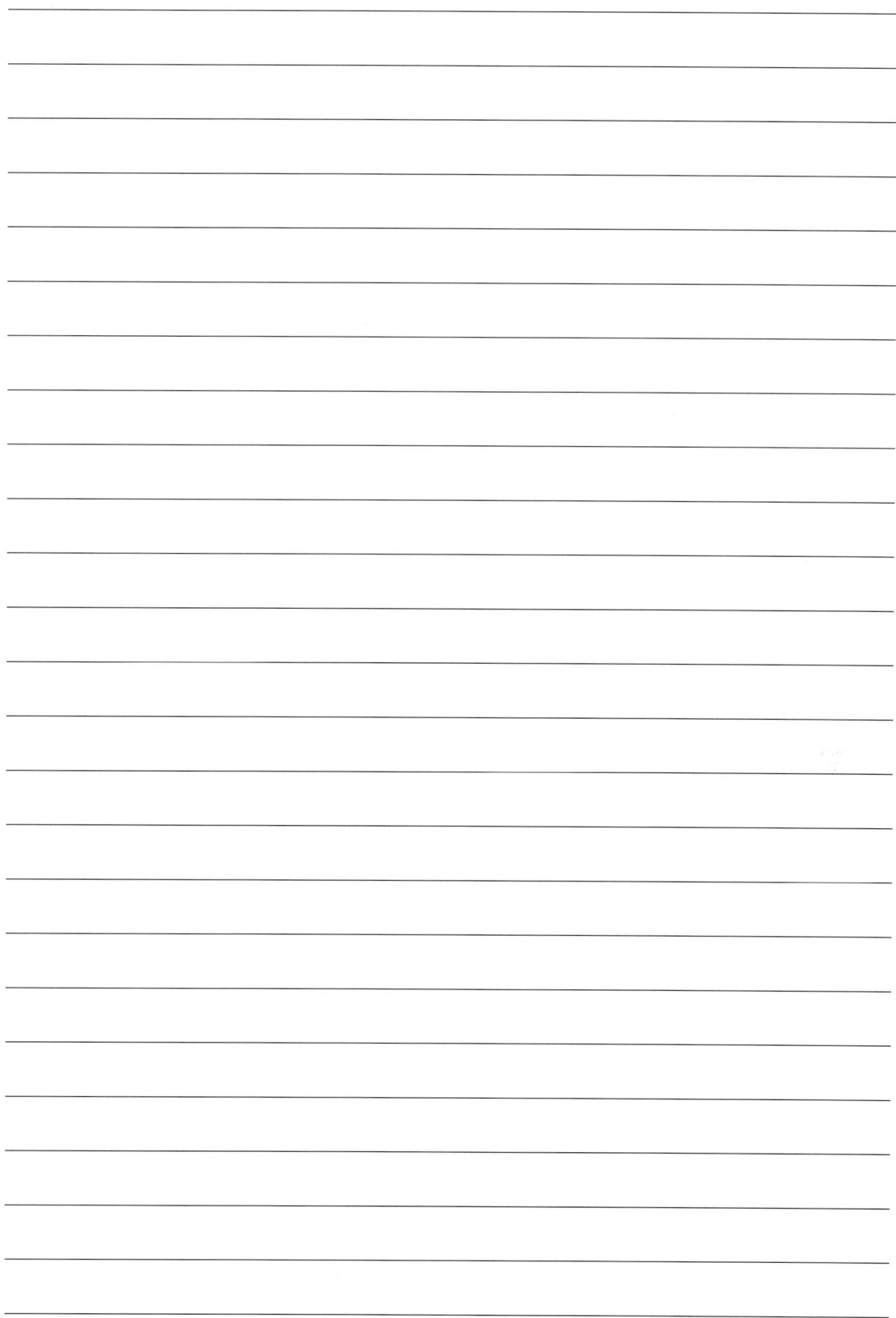

| Date: | Anxiety Scale (1-10): |
	AM PM
Today was I compassionate with myself or critical?	Are my thoughts giving me power or taking it away?

Are my thoughts true? *Really true?*

Am I avoiding something that I need to deal with?

Am I forecasting the future?

Am I "catastrophizing"?

Did I experience fear today?	Did it actually come true?
What helps to ease my anxiety?	Did I remember that?
Did I nourish my body and drink enough water?	Did I get fresh air?
How did I move my body today?	Did I try to practice mindfulness and deep breathing?
Did I have "What if's" today?	I am grateful for:

Promise me you'll always remember:
You're braver than you believe, stronger than you seem and smarter than you think.
A.A. Milne

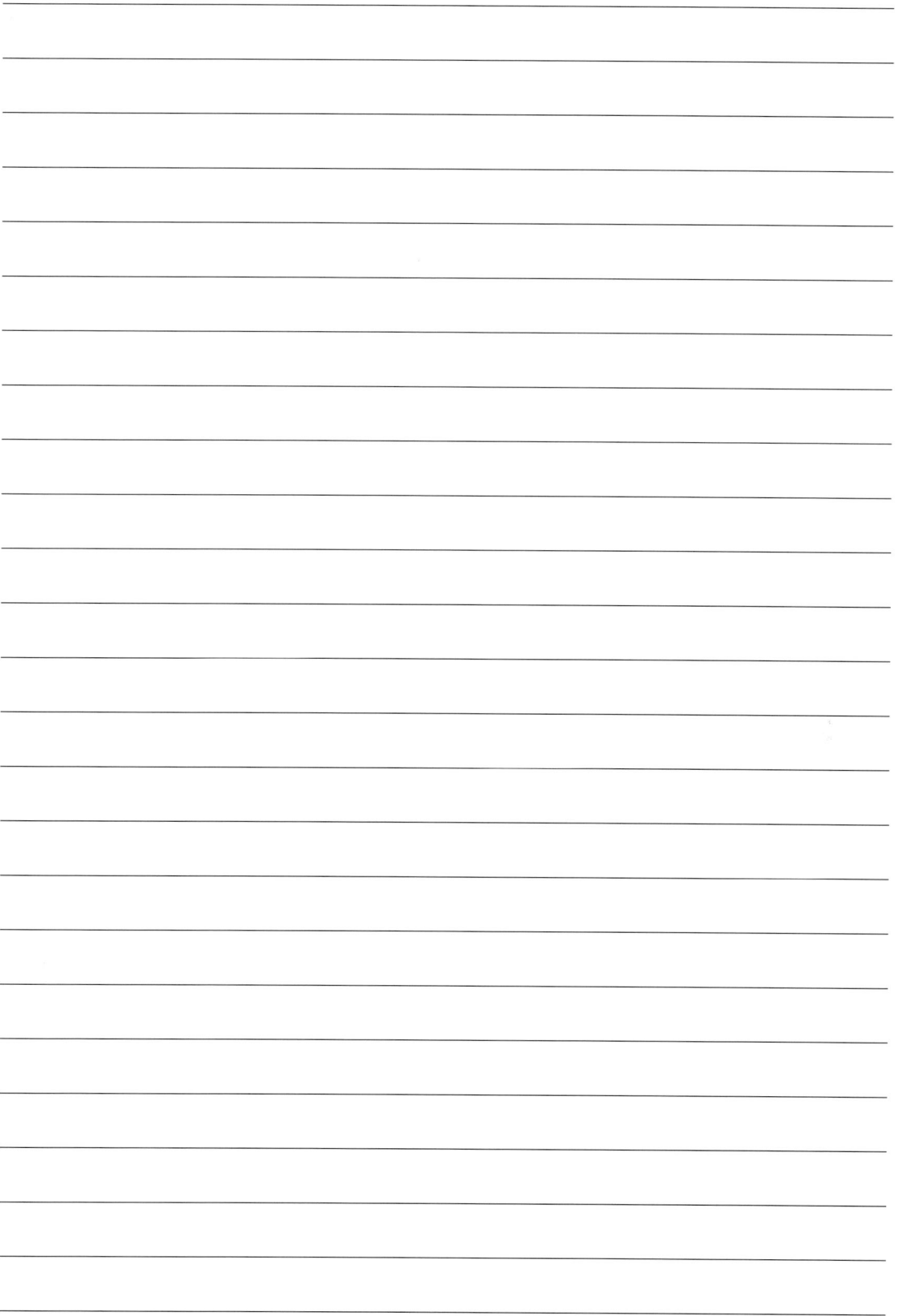

REVIEW OF LAST WEEK

Overall my week was...

Did I have the support I needed? | Did I ask for help when I needed it?

Did I remember my intentions from last week?

Did I spend enough time being unplugged?

I am proud that I....

Notes:

WEEKLY CHECK-IN

My Intention for Next Week:

I would like to:

Experience...

Let go of...

Feel...

Learn to...

Stop...

I want more...	I want less...

Date:	Anxiety Scale (1-10): AM PM
Today was I compassionate with myself or critical?	Are my thoughts giving me power or taking it away?

Are my thoughts true? *Really true?*

Am I avoiding something that I need to deal with?

Am I forecasting the future?

Am I "catastrophizing"?

Did I experience fear today?	Did it actually come true?
What helps to ease my anxiety?	Did I remember that?
Did I nourish my body and drink enough water?	Did I get fresh air?
How did I move my body today?	Did I try to practice mindfulness and deep breathing?
Did I have "What if's" today?	I am grateful for:

Promise me you'll always remember:
You're braver than you believe, stronger than you seem and smarter than you think.
A.A. Milne

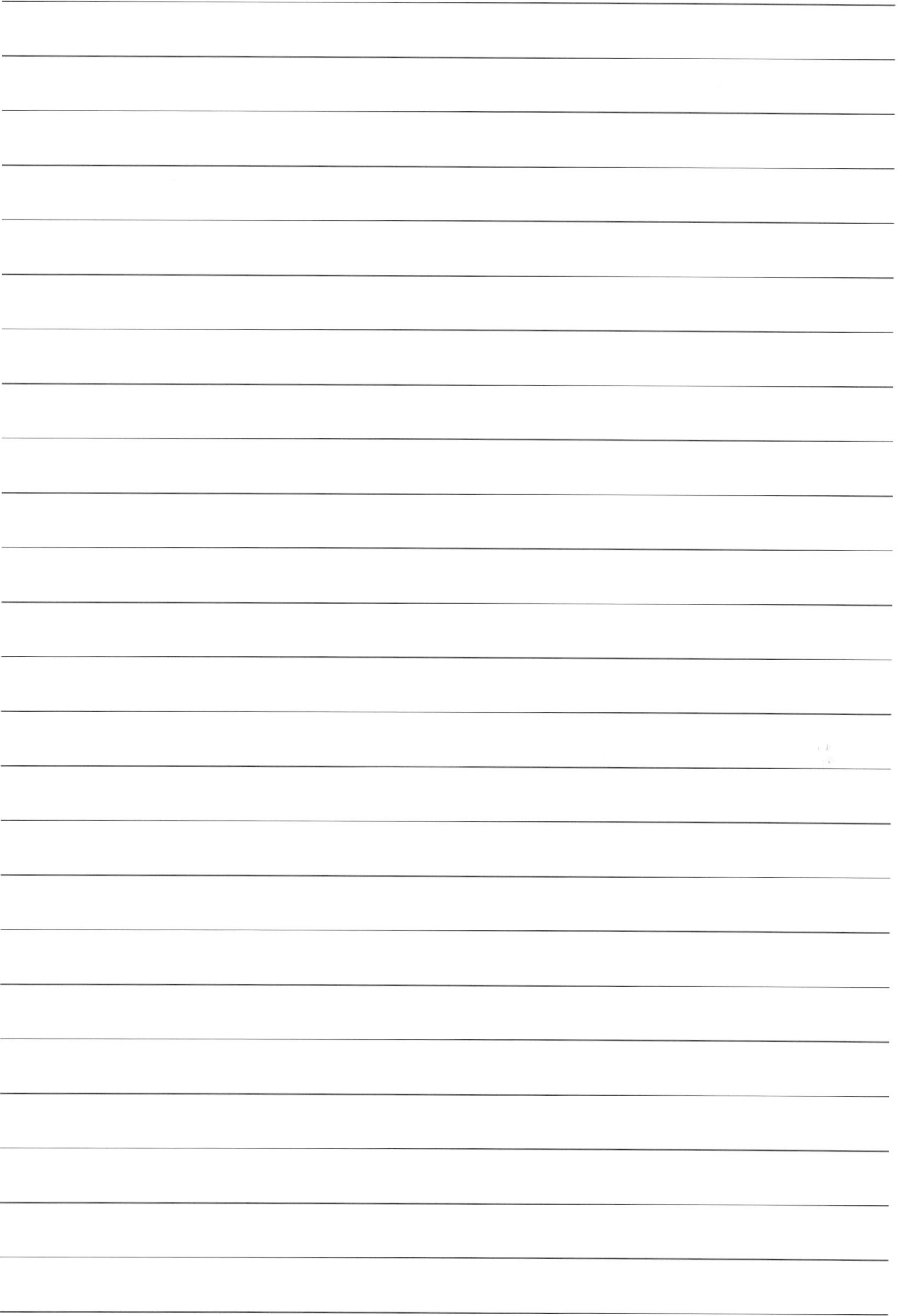

Date:	Anxiety Scale (1-10): AM PM
Today was I compassionate with myself or critical?	Are my thoughts giving me power or taking it away?

Are my thoughts true? *Really true?*

Am I avoiding something that I need to deal with?

Am I forecasting the future?

Am I "catastrophizing"?

Did I experience fear today?	Did it actually come true?
What helps to ease my anxiety?	Did I remember that?
Did I nourish my body and drink enough water?	Did I get fresh air?
How did I move my body today?	Did I try to practice mindfulness and deep breathing?
Did I have "What if's" today?	I am grateful for:

Promise me you'll always remember:
You're braver than you believe, stronger than you seem and smarter than you think.
A.A. Milne

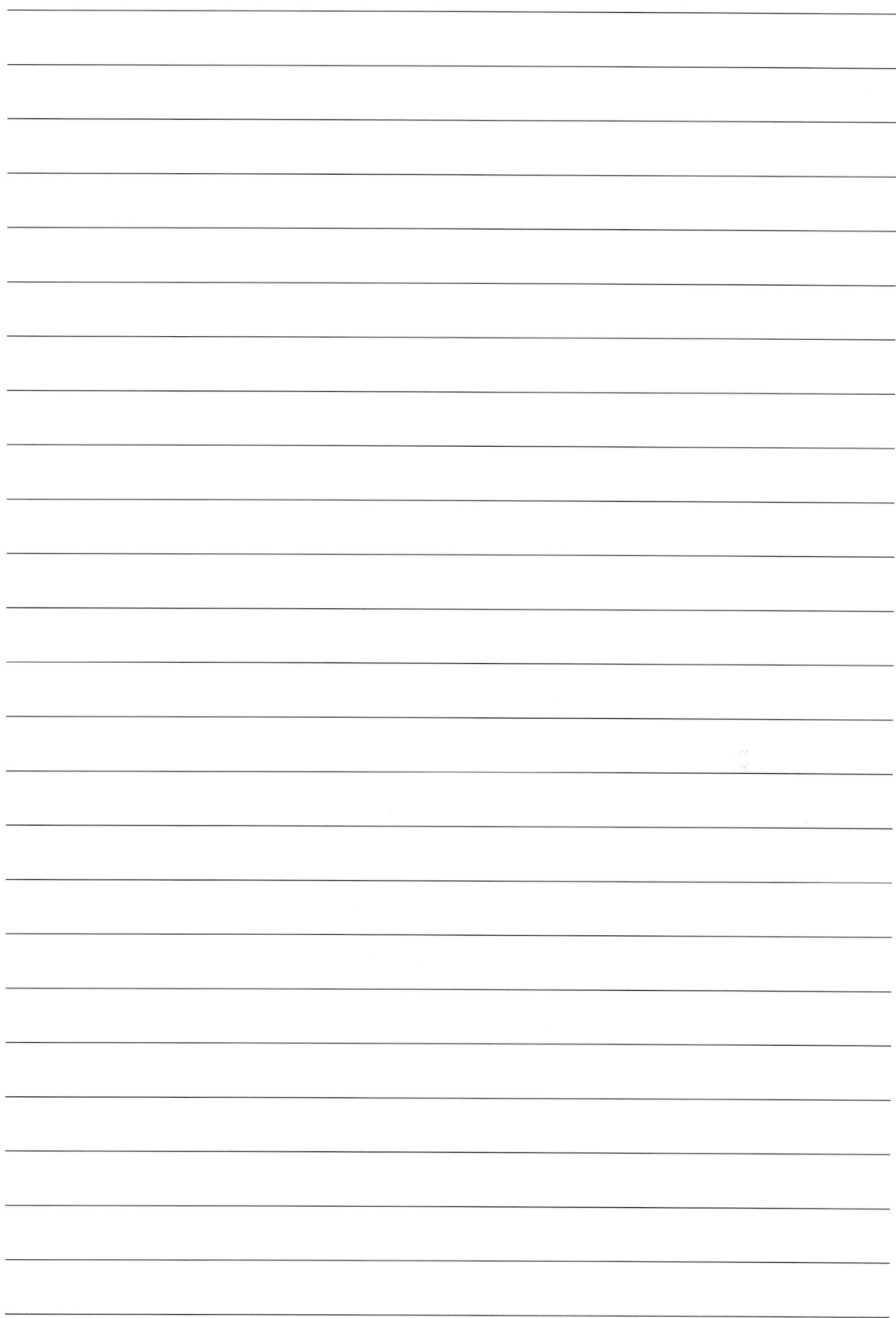

| Date: | Anxiety Scale (1-10): |
| | AM   PM |

| Today was I compassionate with myself or critical? | Are my thoughts giving me power or taking it away? |

Are my thoughts true? *Really true?*

Am I avoiding something that I need to deal with?

Am I forecasting the future?

Am I "catastrophizing"?

| Did I experience fear today? | Did it actually come true? |

| What helps to ease my anxiety? | Did I remember that? |

| Did I nourish my body and drink enough water? | Did I get fresh air? |

| How did I move my body today? | Did I try to practice mindfulness and deep breathing? |

| Did I have "What if's" today? | I am grateful for: |

Promise me you'll always remember:
You're braver than you believe, stronger than you seem and smarter than you think.
A.A. Milne

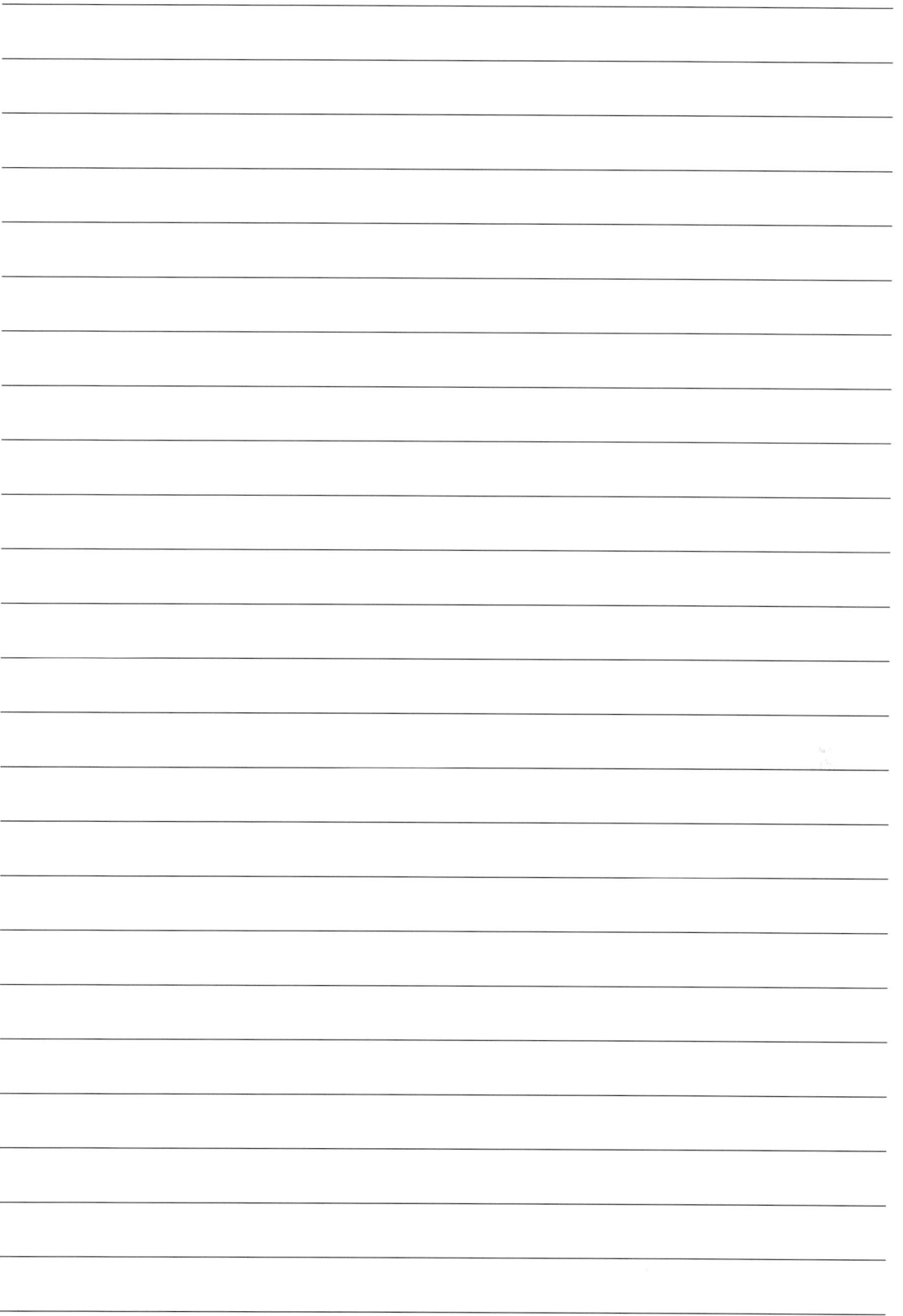

Date:	Anxiety Scale (1-10): AM PM
Today was I compassionate with myself or critical?	Are my thoughts giving me power or taking it away?

Are my thoughts true? *Really true?*

Am I avoiding something that I need to deal with?

Am I forecasting the future?

Am I "catastrophizing"?

Did I experience fear today?	Did it actually come true?
What helps to ease my anxiety?	Did I remember that?
Did I nourish my body and drink enough water?	Did I get fresh air?
How did I move my body today?	Did I try to practice mindfulness and deep breathing?
Did I have "What if's" today?	I am grateful for:

Promise me you'll always remember:
You're braver than you believe, stronger than you seem and smarter than you think.
A.A. Milne

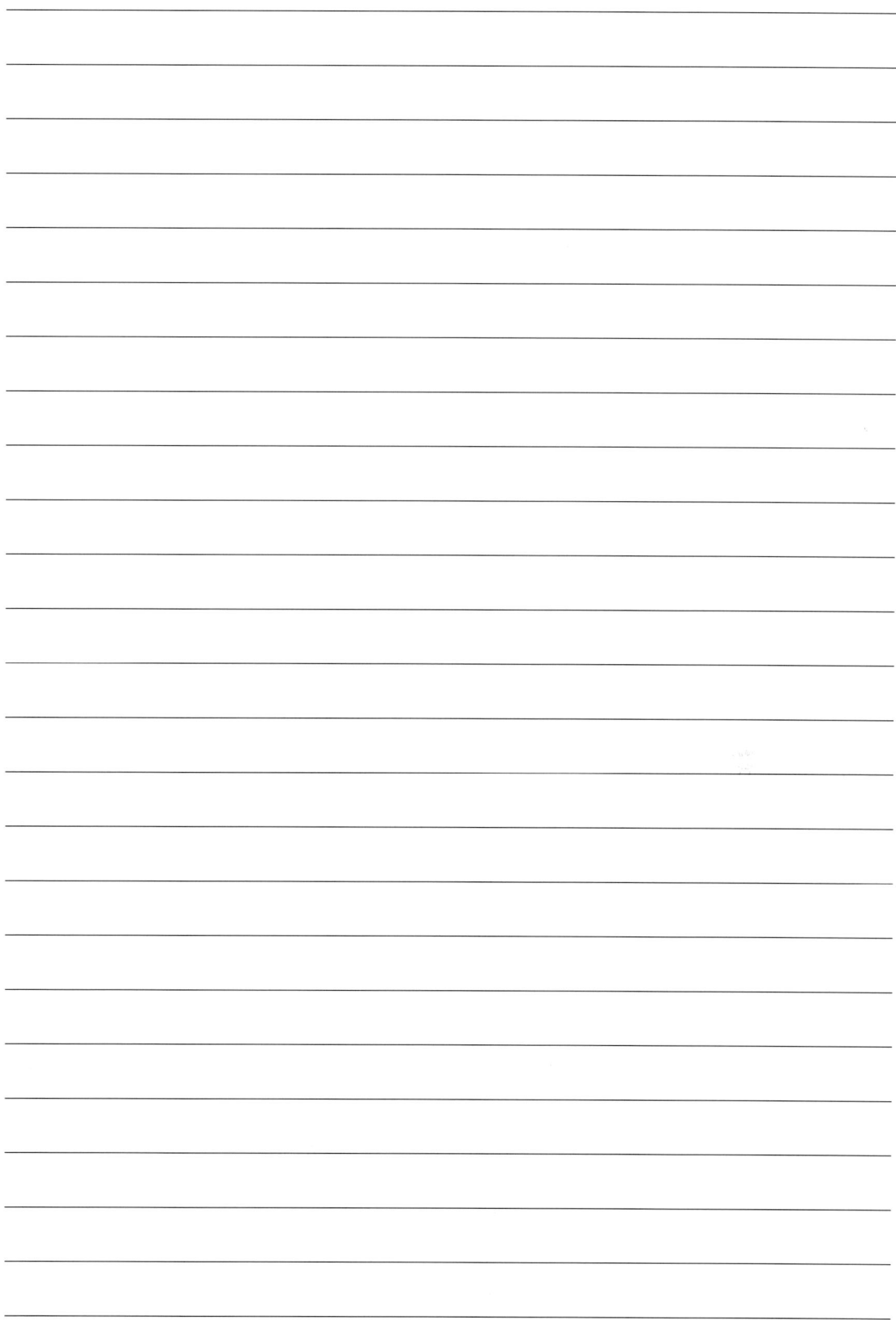

Date:	Anxiety Scale (1-10): AM PM
Today was I compassionate with myself or critical?	Are my thoughts giving me power or taking it away?

Are my thoughts true? *Really true?*

Am I avoiding something that I need to deal with?

Am I forecasting the future?

Am I "catastrophizing"?

Did I experience fear today?	Did it actually come true?
What helps to ease my anxiety?	Did I remember that?
Did I nourish my body and drink enough water?	Did I get fresh air?
How did I move my body today?	Did I try to practice mindfulness and deep breathing?
Did I have "What if's" today?	I am grateful for:

Promise me you'll always remember:
You're braver than you believe, stronger than you seem and smarter than you think.
A.A. Milne

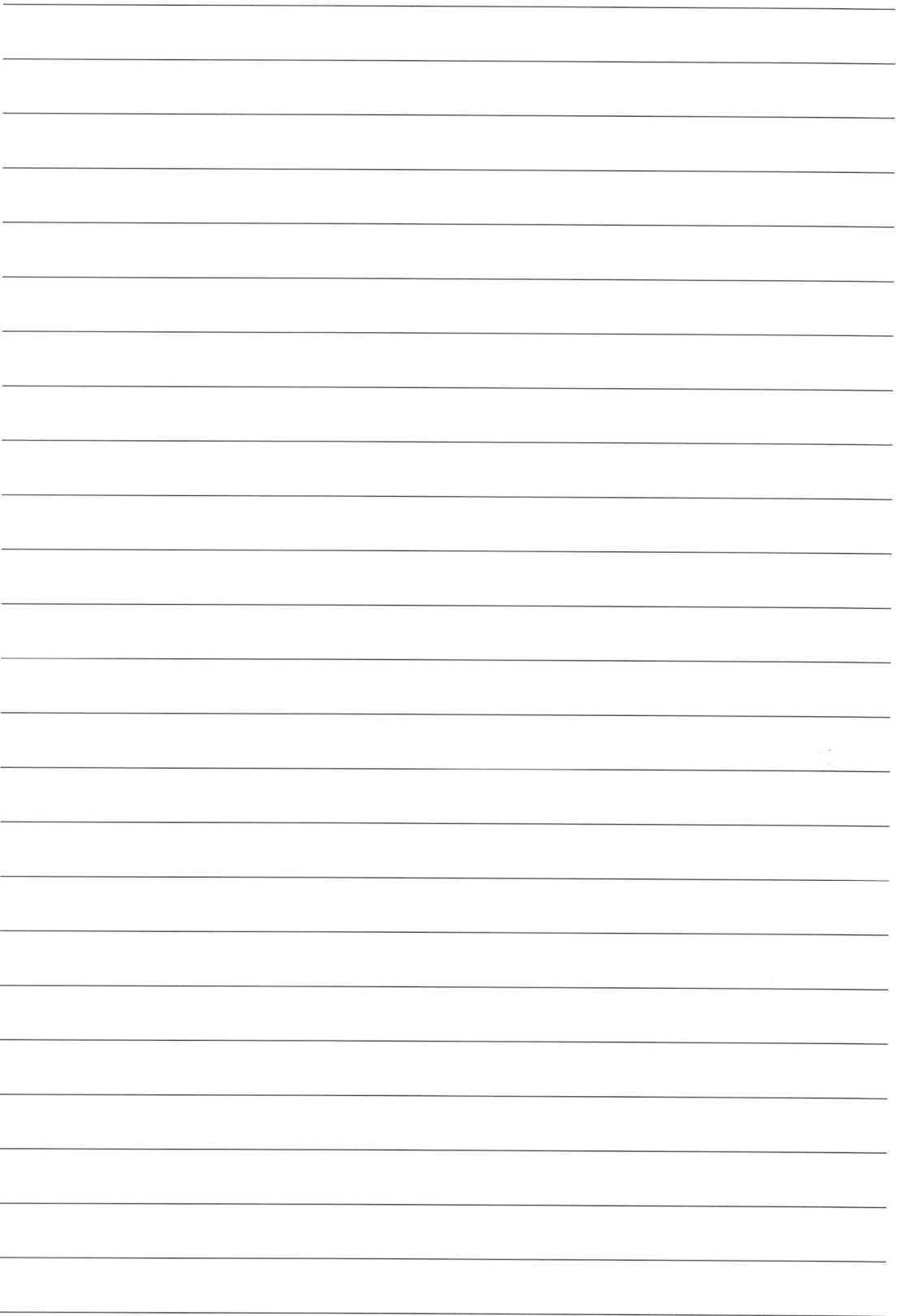

Date:	Anxiety Scale (1-10): AM PM
Today was I compassionate with myself or critical?	Are my thoughts giving me power or taking it away?

Are my thoughts true? *Really true?*

Am I avoiding something that I need to deal with?

Am I forecasting the future?

Am I "catastrophizing"?

Did I experience fear today?	Did it actually come true?
What helps to ease my anxiety?	Did I remember that?
Did I nourish my body and drink enough water?	Did I get fresh air?
How did I move my body today?	Did I try to practice mindfulness and deep breathing?
Did I have "What if's" today?	I am grateful for:

Promise me you'll always remember:
You're braver than you believe, stronger than you seem and smarter than you think.
A.A. Milne

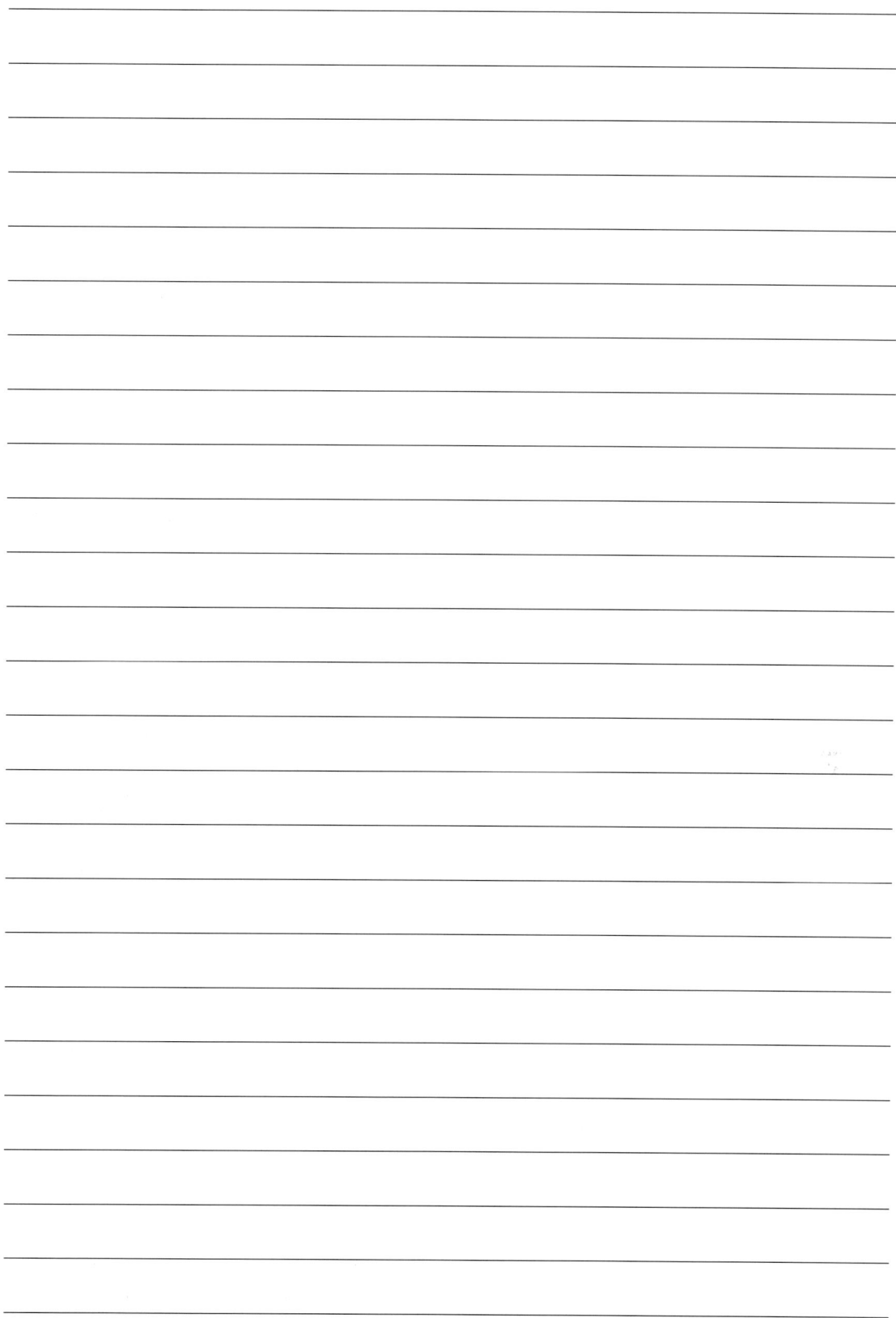

Date:	Anxiety Scale (1-10): AM PM
Today was I compassionate with myself or critical?	Are my thoughts giving me power or taking it away?

Are my thoughts true? *Really true?*

Am I avoiding something that I need to deal with?

Am I forecasting the future?

Am I "catastrophizing"?

Did I experience fear today?	Did it actually come true?
What helps to ease my anxiety?	Did I remember that?
Did I nourish my body and drink enough water?	Did I get fresh air?
How did I move my body today?	Did I try to practice mindfulness and deep breathing?
Did I have "What if's" today?	I am grateful for:

Promise me you'll always remember:
You're braver than you believe, stronger than you seem and smarter than you think.
A.A. Milne

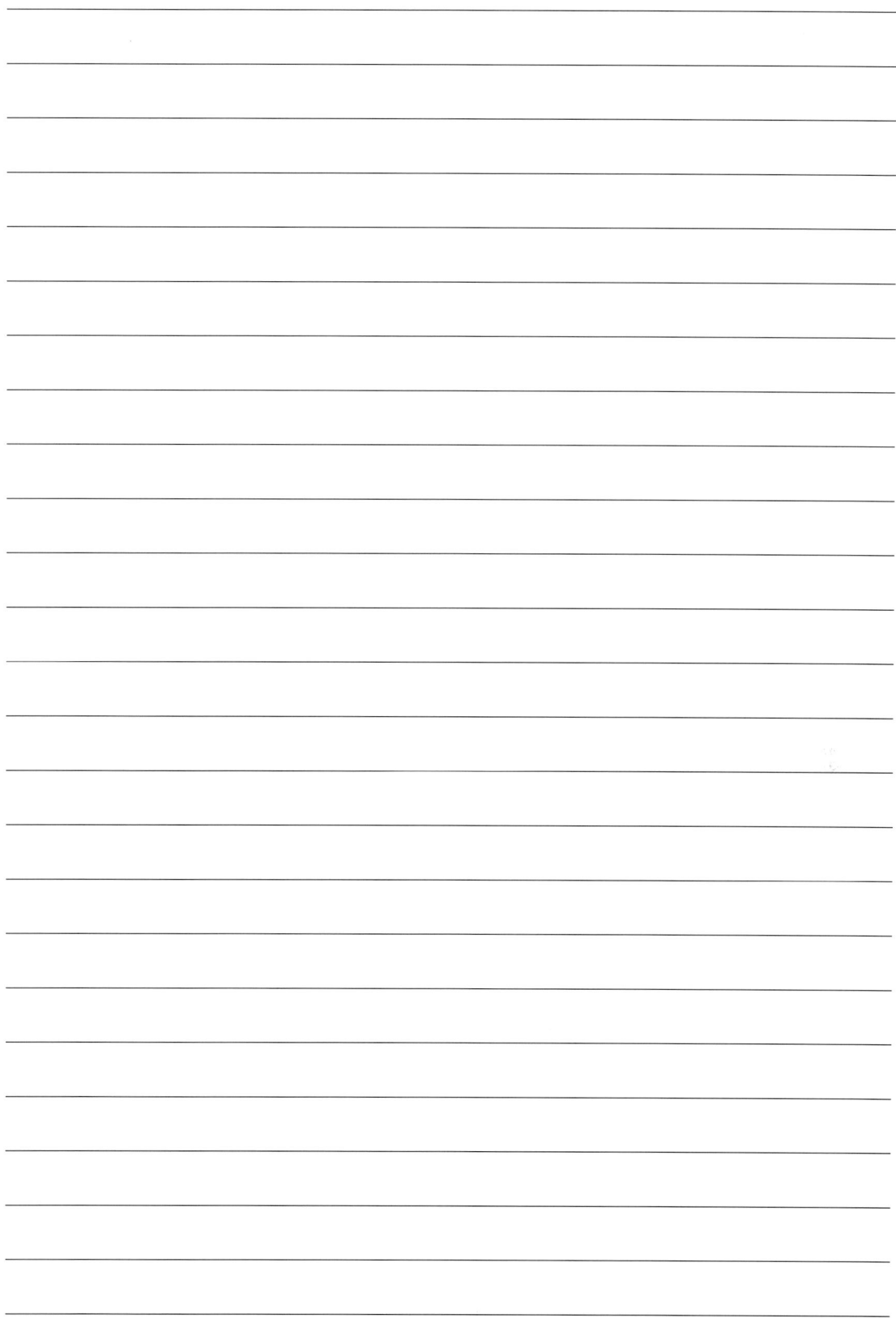

REVIEW OF LAST WEEK

Overall my week was...

Did I have the support I needed? | Did I ask for help when I needed it?

Did I remember my intentions from last week?

Did I spend enough time being unplugged?

I am proud that I....

Notes:

WEEKLY CHECK-IN

My Intention for Next Week:

I would like to:

Experience...

Let go of...

Feel...

Learn to...

Stop...

I want more...	I want less...

Date:	Anxiety Scale (1-10): AM PM
Today was I compassionate with myself or critical?	Are my thoughts giving me power or taking it away?

Are my thoughts true? *Really true?*

Am I avoiding something that I need to deal with?

Am I forecasting the future?

Am I "catastrophizing"?

Did I experience fear today?	Did it actually come true?
What helps to ease my anxiety?	Did I remember that?
Did I nourish my body and drink enough water?	Did I get fresh air?
How did I move my body today?	Did I try to practice mindfulness and deep breathing?
Did I have "What if's" today?	I am grateful for:

Promise me you'll always remember:
You're braver than you believe, stronger than you seem and smarter than you think.
A.A. Milne

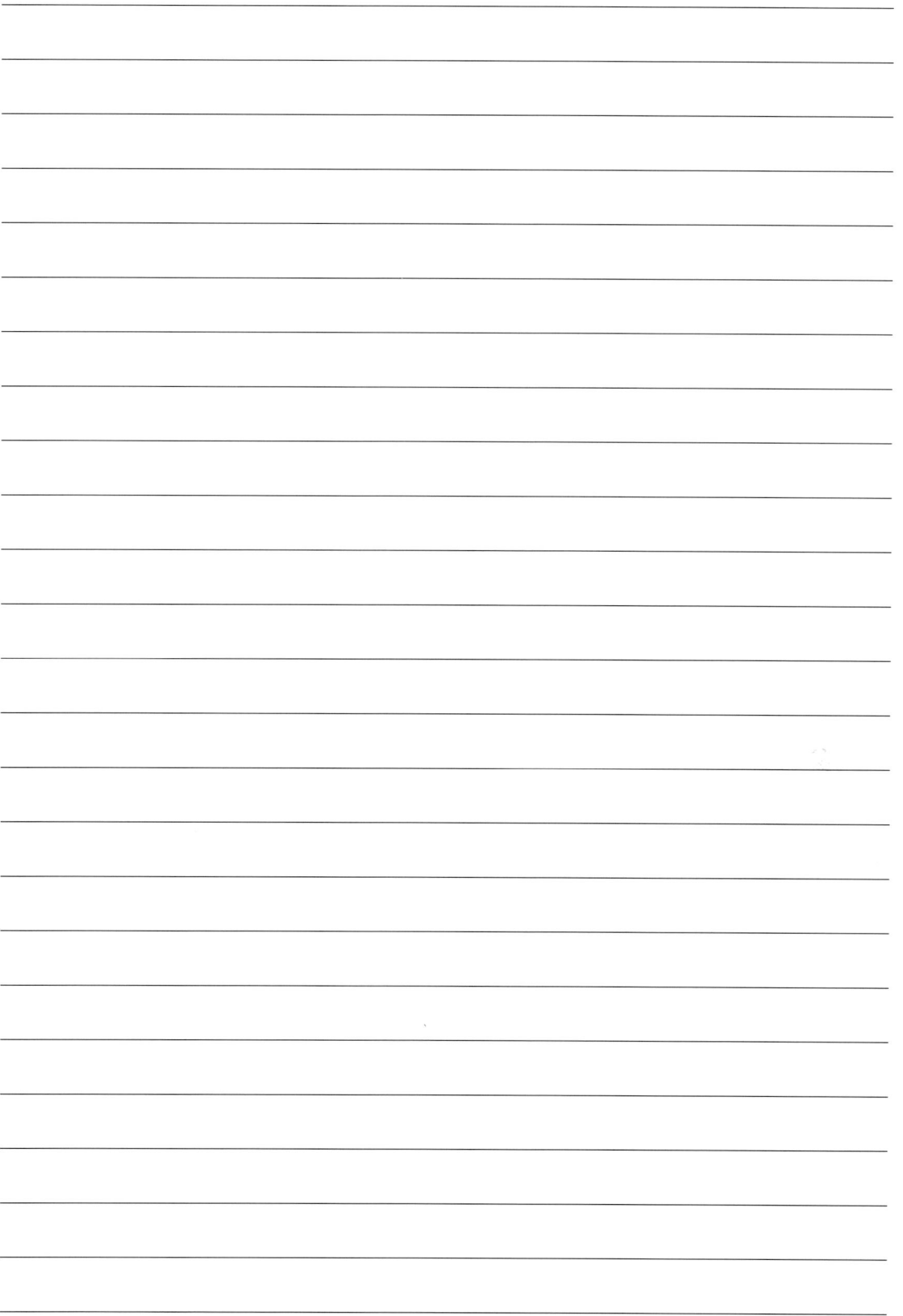

Date:	Anxiety Scale (1-10): AM PM
Today was I compassionate with myself or critical?	Are my thoughts giving me power or taking it away?

Are my thoughts true? *Really true?*

Am I avoiding something that I need to deal with?

Am I forecasting the future?

Am I "catastrophizing"?

Did I experience fear today?	Did it actually come true?
What helps to ease my anxiety?	Did I remember that?
Did I nourish my body and drink enough water?	Did I get fresh air?
How did I move my body today?	Did I try to practice mindfulness and deep breathing?
Did I have "What if's" today?	I am grateful for:

Promise me you'll always remember:
You're braver than you believe, stronger than you seem and smarter than you think.
A.A. Milne

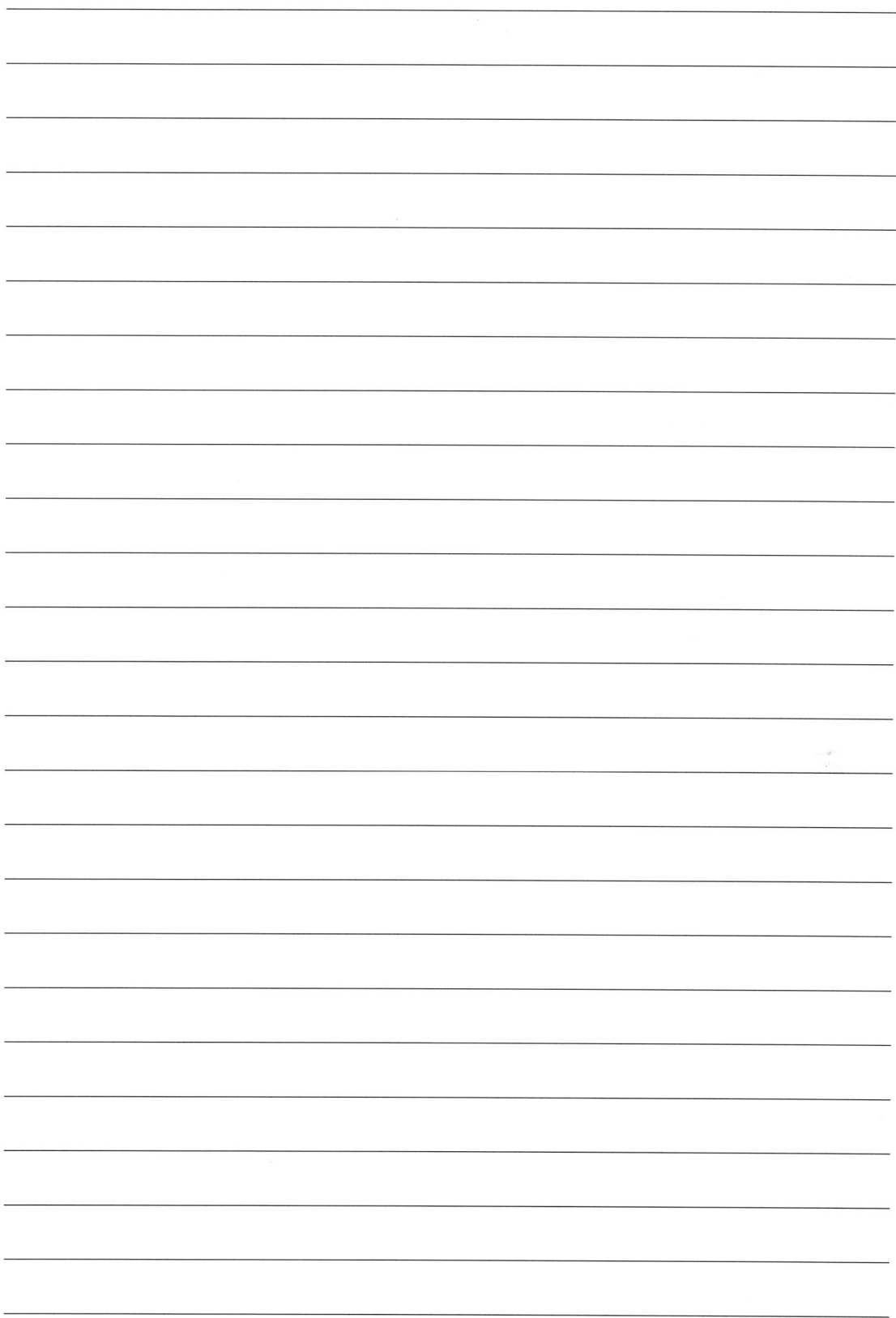

Date:	Anxiety Scale (1-10): AM PM
Today was I compassionate with myself or critical?	Are my thoughts giving me power or taking it away?

Are my thoughts true? *Really true?*

Am I avoiding something that I need to deal with?

Am I forecasting the future?

Am I "catastrophizing"?

Did I experience fear today?	Did it actually come true?
What helps to ease my anxiety?	Did I remember that?
Did I nourish my body and drink enough water?	Did I get fresh air?
How did I move my body today?	Did I try to practice mindfulness and deep breathing?
Did I have "What if's" today?	I am grateful for:

Promise me you'll always remember:
You're braver than you believe, stronger than you seem and smarter than you think.
A.A. Milne

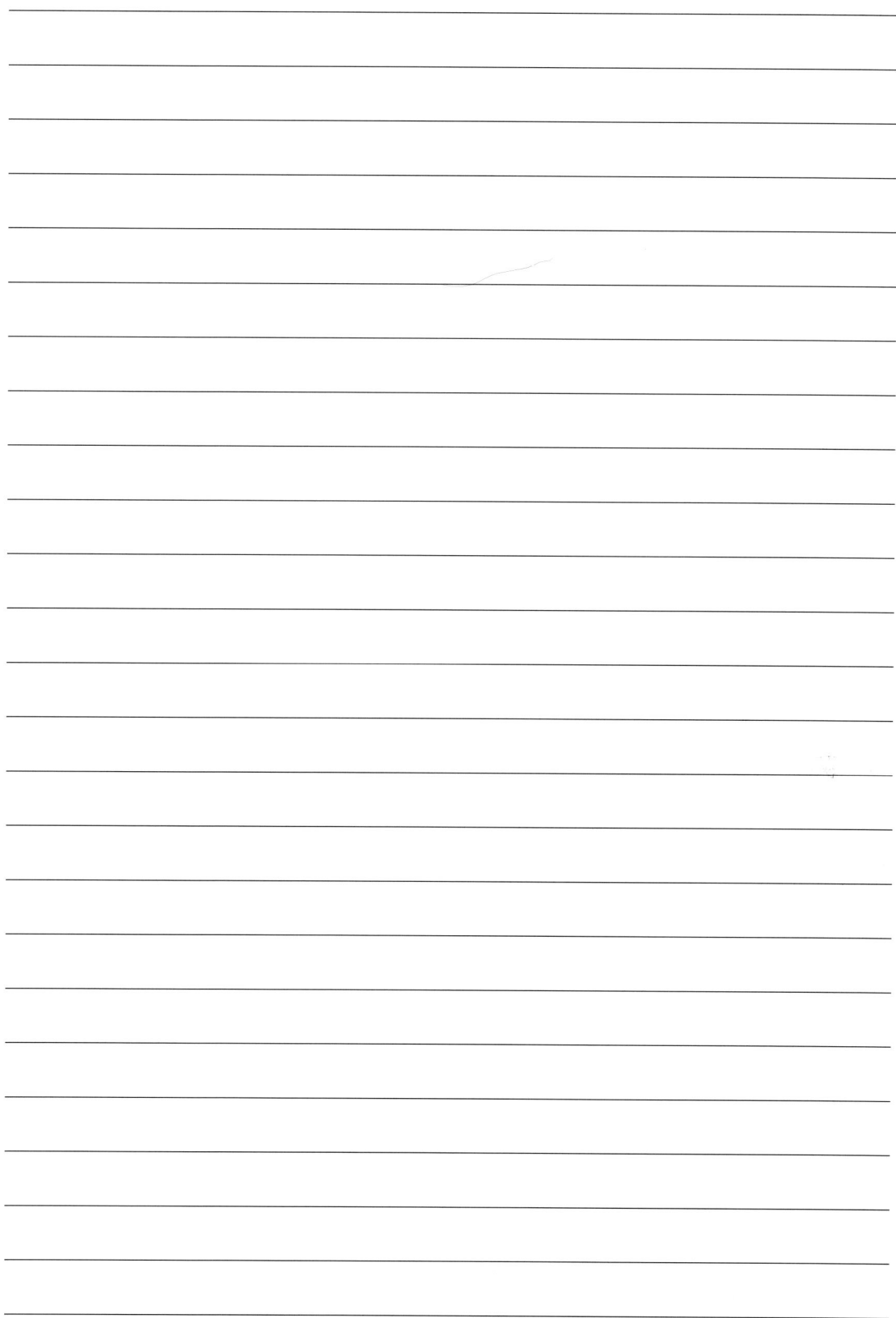

Date:	Anxiety Scale (1-10): AM PM
Today was I compassionate with myself or critical?	Are my thoughts giving me power or taking it away?

Are my thoughts true? *Really true?*

Am I avoiding something that I need to deal with?

Am I forecasting the future?

Am I "catastrophizing"?

Did I experience fear today?	Did it actually come true?
What helps to ease my anxiety?	Did I remember that?
Did I nourish my body and drink enough water?	Did I get fresh air?
How did I move my body today?	Did I try to practice mindfulness and deep breathing?
Did I have "What if's" today?	I am grateful for:

Promise me you'll always remember:
You're braver than you believe, stronger than you seem and smarter than you think.
A.A. Milne

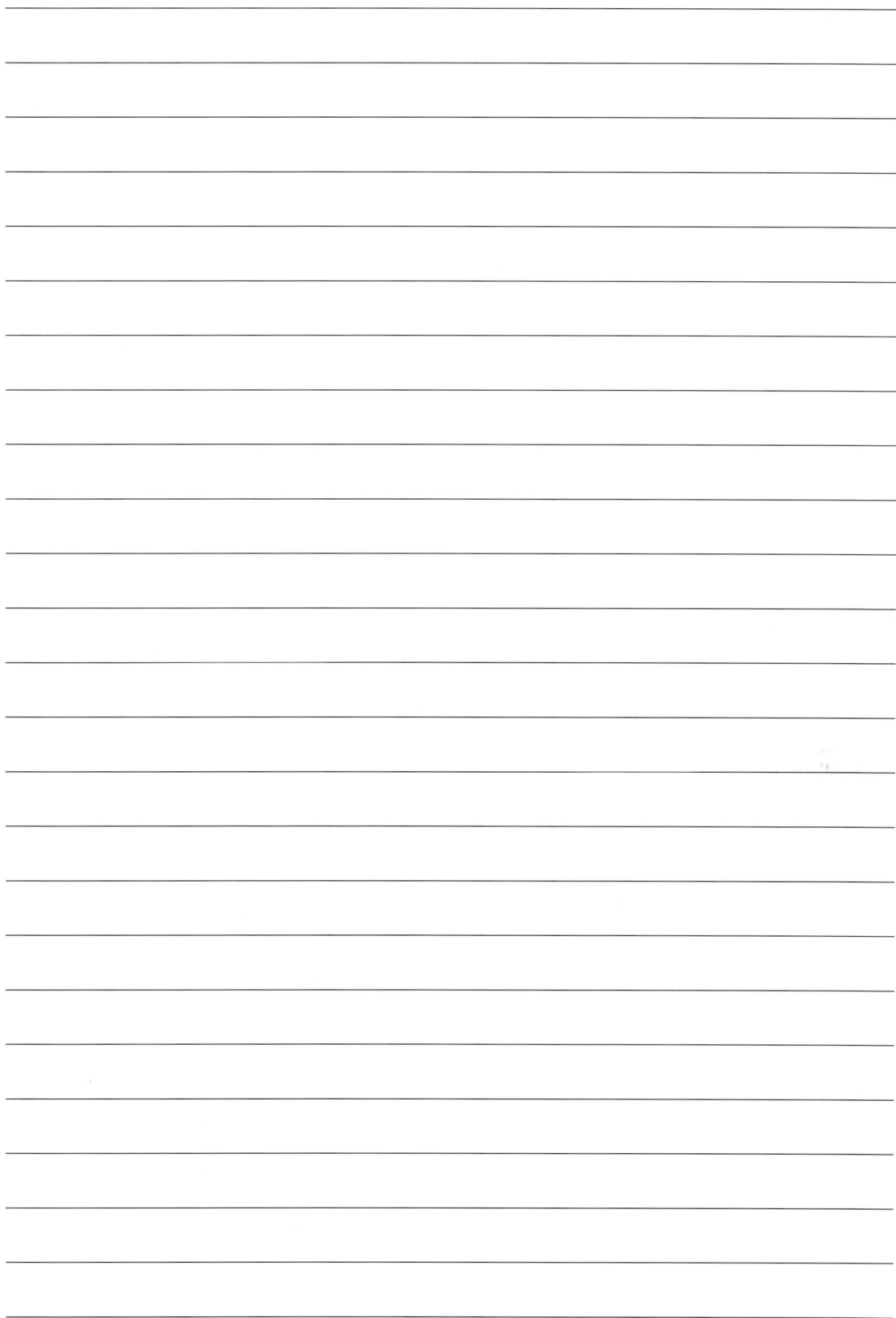

Date:	Anxiety Scale (1-10): AM PM
Today was I compassionate with myself or critical?	Are my thoughts giving me power or taking it away?

Are my thoughts true? *Really true?*

Am I avoiding something that I need to deal with?

Am I forecasting the future?

Am I "catastrophizing"?

Did I experience fear today?	Did it actually come true?
What helps to ease my anxiety?	Did I remember that?
Did I nourish my body and drink enough water?	Did I get fresh air?
How did I move my body today?	Did I try to practice mindfulness and deep breathing?
Did I have "What if's" today?	I am grateful for:

Promise me you'll always remember:
You're braver than you believe, stronger than you seem and smarter than you think.
A.A. Milne

Date:	Anxiety Scale (1-10): AM PM
Today was I compassionate with myself or critical?	Are my thoughts giving me power or taking it away?

Are my thoughts true? *Really true?*

Am I avoiding something that I need to deal with?

Am I forecasting the future?

Am I "catastrophizing"?

Did I experience fear today?	Did it actually come true?
What helps to ease my anxiety?	Did I remember that?
Did I nourish my body and drink enough water?	Did I get fresh air?
How did I move my body today?	Did I try to practice mindfulness and deep breathing?
Did I have "What if's" today?	I am grateful for:

Promise me you'll always remember:
You're braver than you believe, stronger than you seem and smarter than you think.
A.A. Milne

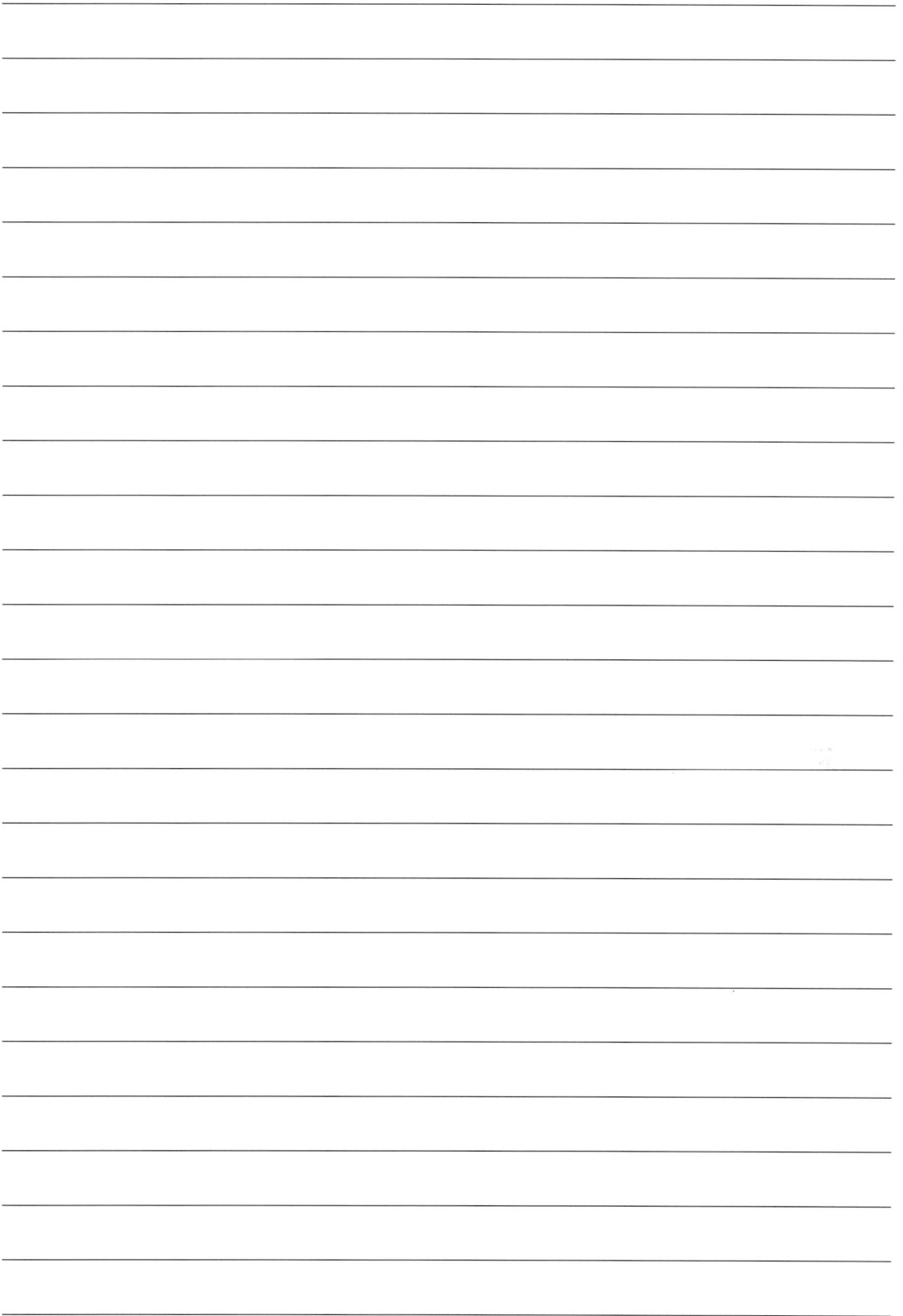

Date:	Anxiety Scale (1-10): AM PM
Today was I compassionate with myself or critical?	Are my thoughts giving me power or taking it away?

Are my thoughts true? *Really true?*

Am I avoiding something that I need to deal with?

Am I forecasting the future?

Am I "catastrophizing"?

Did I experience fear today?	Did it actually come true?
What helps to ease my anxiety?	Did I remember that?
Did I nourish my body and drink enough water?	Did I get fresh air?
How did I move my body today?	Did I try to practice mindfulness and deep breathing?
Did I have "What if's" today?	I am grateful for:

Promise me you'll always remember:
You're braver than you believe, stronger than you seem and smarter than you think.
A.A. Milne

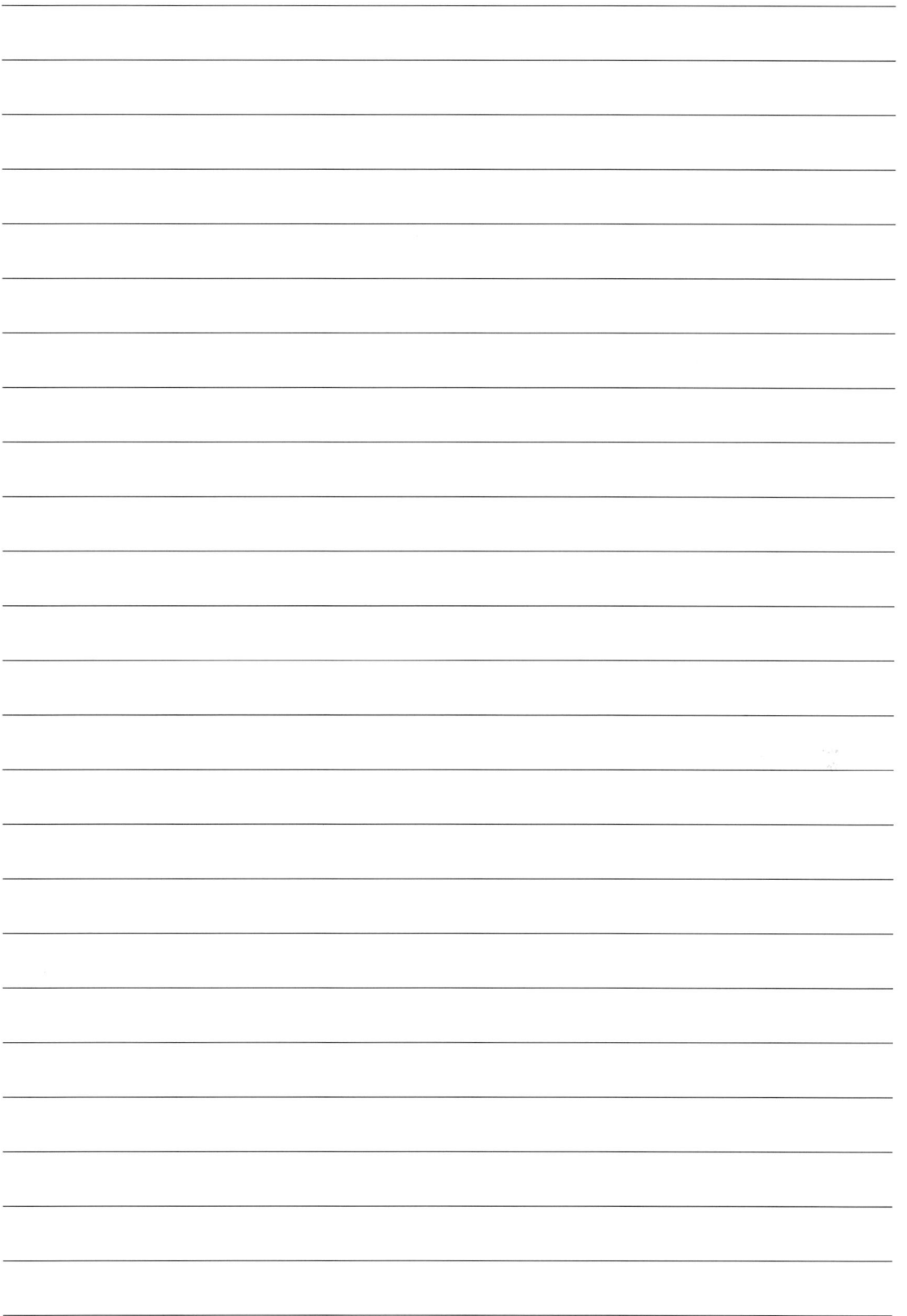

REVIEW OF LAST WEEK

Overall my week was...

Did I have the support I needed?	Did I ask for help when I needed it?

Did I remember my intentions from last week?

Did I spend enough time being unplugged?

I am proud that I....

Notes:

WEEKLY CHECK-IN

My Intention for Next Week:

I would like to:

Experience...

Let go of...

Feel...

Learn to...

Stop...

I want more...	I want less...

Date:	Anxiety Scale (1-10): AM PM
Today was I compassionate with myself or critical?	Are my thoughts giving me power or taking it away?

Are my thoughts true? *Really true?*

Am I avoiding something that I need to deal with?

Am I forecasting the future?

Am I "catastrophizing"?

Did I experience fear today?	Did it actually come true?
What helps to ease my anxiety?	Did I remember that?
Did I nourish my body and drink enough water?	Did I get fresh air?
How did I move my body today?	Did I try to practice mindfulness and deep breathing?
Did I have "What if's" today?	I am grateful for:

Promise me you'll always remember:
You're braver than you believe, stronger than you seem and smarter than you think.
A.A. Milne

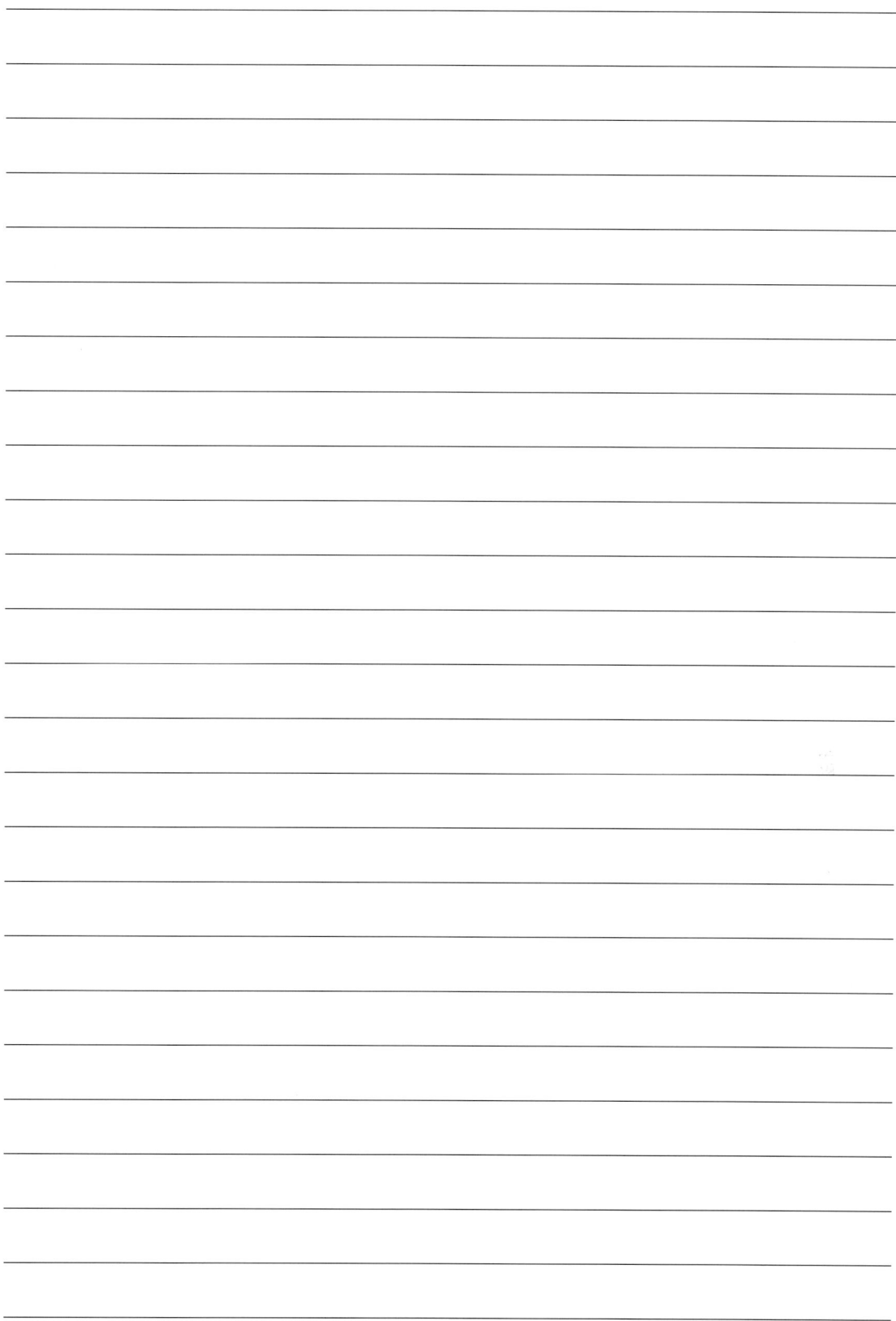

| Date: | Anxiety Scale (1-10): |
	AM PM
Today was I compassionate with myself or critical?	Are my thoughts giving me power or taking it away?

Are my thoughts true? *Really true?*

Am I avoiding something that I need to deal with?

Am I forecasting the future?

Am I "catastrophizing"?

Did I experience fear today?	Did it actually come true?
What helps to ease my anxiety?	Did I remember that?
Did I nourish my body and drink enough water?	Did I get fresh air?
How did I move my body today?	Did I try to practice mindfulness and deep breathing?
Did I have "What if's" today?	I am grateful for:

Promise me you'll always remember:
You're braver than you believe, stronger than you seem and smarter than you think.
A.A. Milne

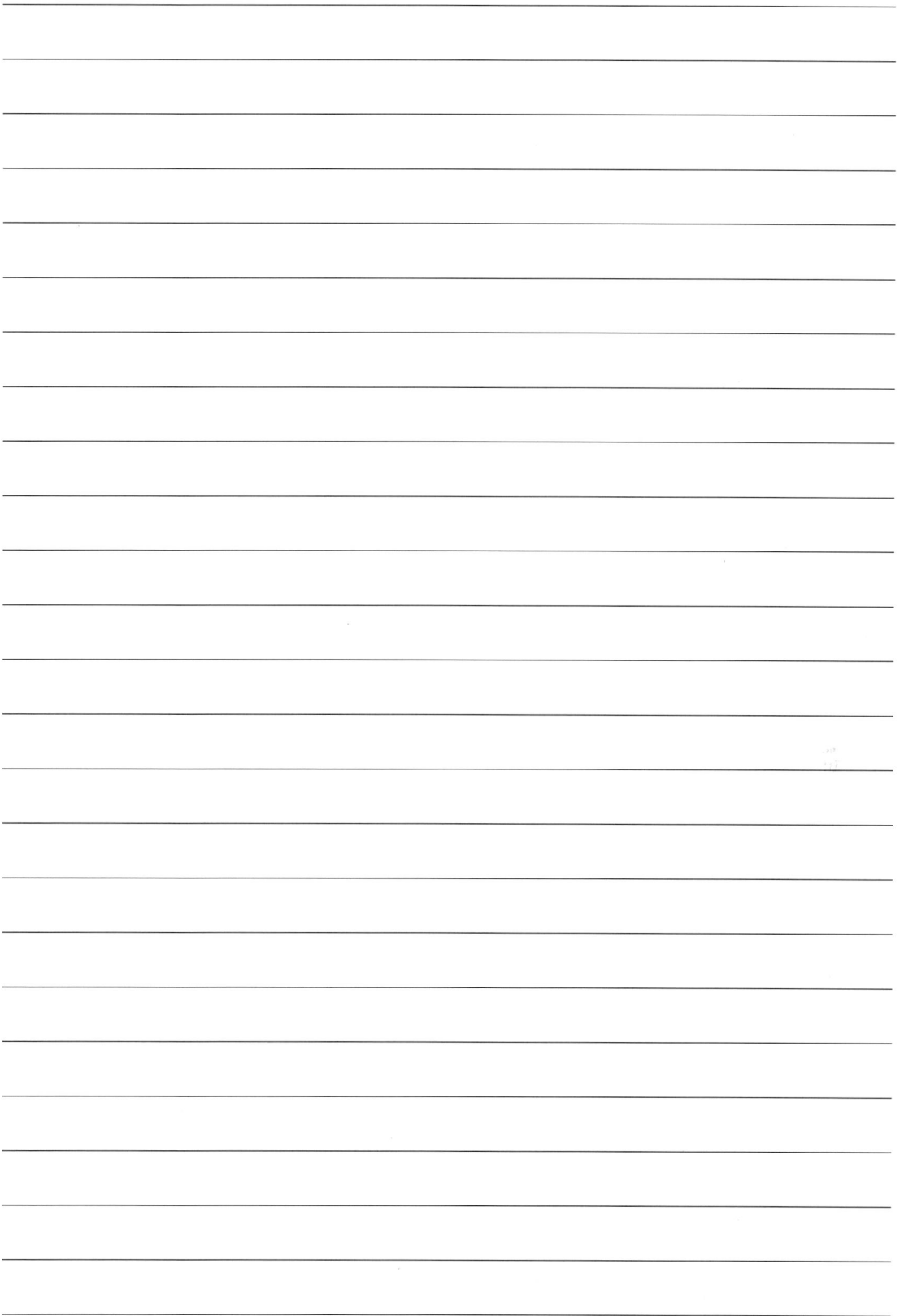

Date:	Anxiety Scale (1-10): AM PM
Today was I compassionate with myself or critical?	Are my thoughts giving me power or taking it away?

Are my thoughts true? *Really true?*

Am I avoiding something that I need to deal with?

Am I forecasting the future?

Am I "catastrophizing"?

Did I experience fear today?	Did it actually come true?
What helps to ease my anxiety?	Did I remember that?
Did I nourish my body and drink enough water?	Did I get fresh air?
How did I move my body today?	Did I try to practice mindfulness and deep breathing?
Did I have "What if's" today?	I am grateful for:

Promise me you'll always remember:
You're braver than you believe, stronger than you seem and smarter than you think.
A.A. Milne

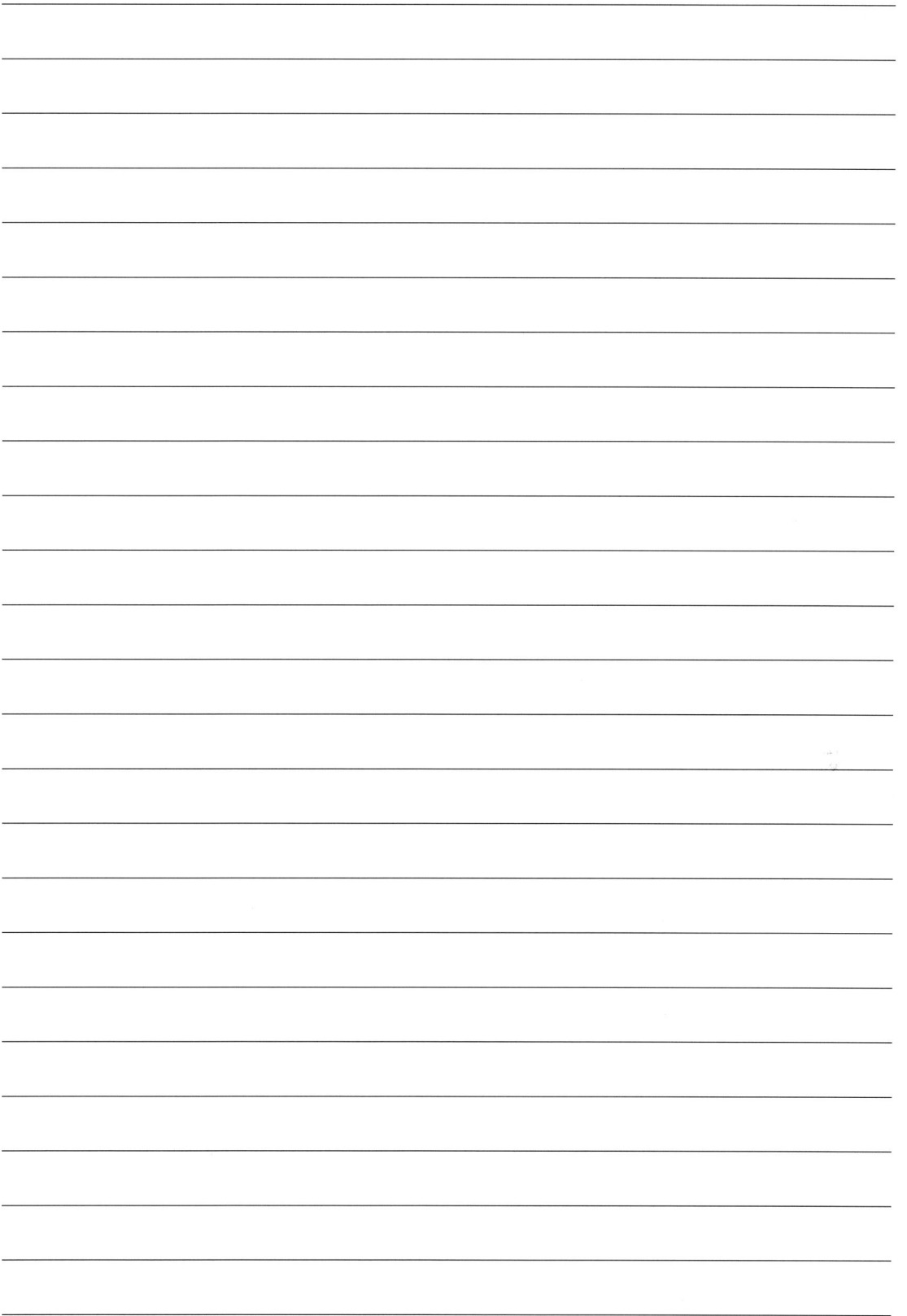

Date:	Anxiety Scale (1-10): AM PM
Today was I compassionate with myself or critical?	Are my thoughts giving me power or taking it away?

Are my thoughts true? *Really true?*

Am I avoiding something that I need to deal with?

Am I forecasting the future?

Am I "catastrophizing"?

Did I experience fear today?	Did it actually come true?
What helps to ease my anxiety?	Did I remember that?
Did I nourish my body and drink enough water?	Did I get fresh air?
How did I move my body today?	Did I try to practice mindfulness and deep breathing?
Did I have "What if's" today?	I am grateful for:

Promise me you'll always remember:
You're braver than you believe, stronger than you seem and smarter than you think.
A.A. Milne

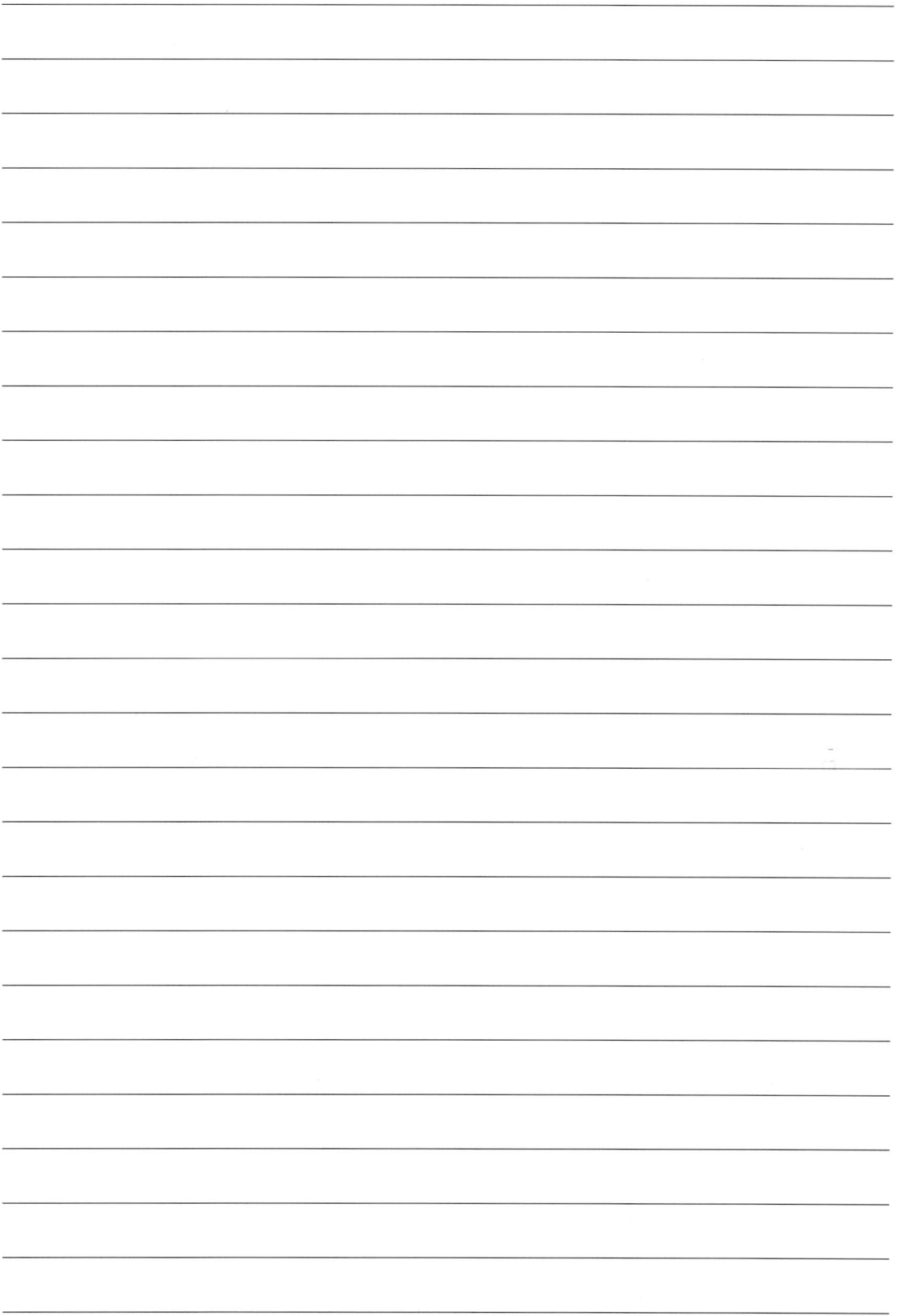

Date:	Anxiety Scale (1-10): AM PM
Today was I compassionate with myself or critical?	Are my thoughts giving me power or taking it away?

Are my thoughts true? *Really true?*

Am I avoiding something that I need to deal with?

Am I forecasting the future?

Am I "catastrophizing"?

Did I experience fear today?	Did it actually come true?
What helps to ease my anxiety?	Did I remember that?
Did I nourish my body and drink enough water?	Did I get fresh air?
How did I move my body today?	Did I try to practice mindfulness and deep breathing?
Did I have "What if's" today?	I am grateful for:

Promise me you'll always remember:
You're braver than you believe, stronger than you seem and smarter than you think.
A.A. Milne

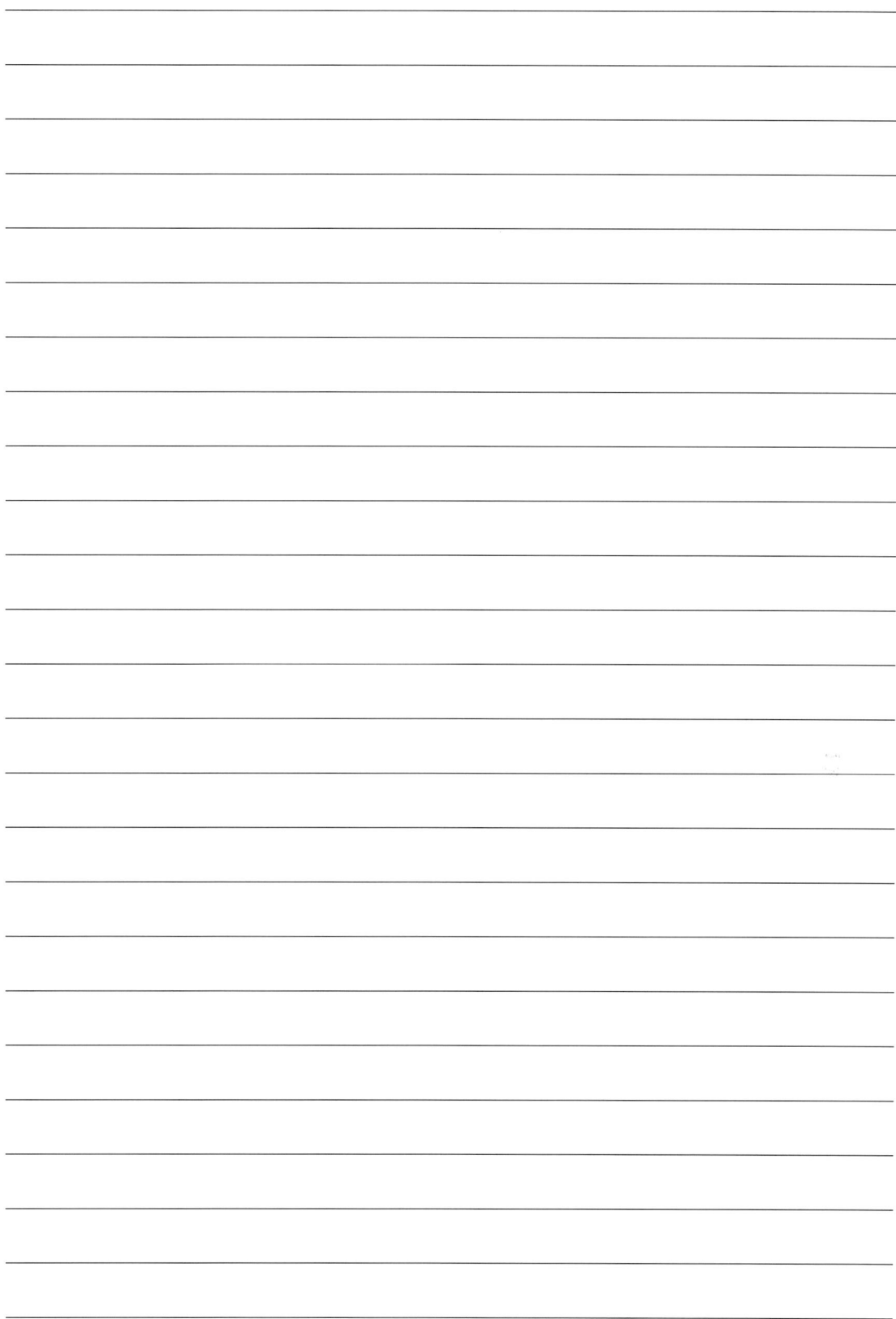

Date:	Anxiety Scale (1-10): AM PM
Today was I compassionate with myself or critical?	Are my thoughts giving me power or taking it away?

Are my thoughts true? *Really true?*

Am I avoiding something that I need to deal with?

Am I forecasting the future?

Am I "catastrophizing"?

Did I experience fear today?	Did it actually come true?
What helps to ease my anxiety?	Did I remember that?
Did I nourish my body and drink enough water?	Did I get fresh air?
How did I move my body today?	Did I try to practice mindfulness and deep breathing?
Did I have "What if's" today?	I am grateful for:

Promise me you'll always remember:
You're braver than you believe, stronger than you seem and smarter than you think.
A.A. Milne

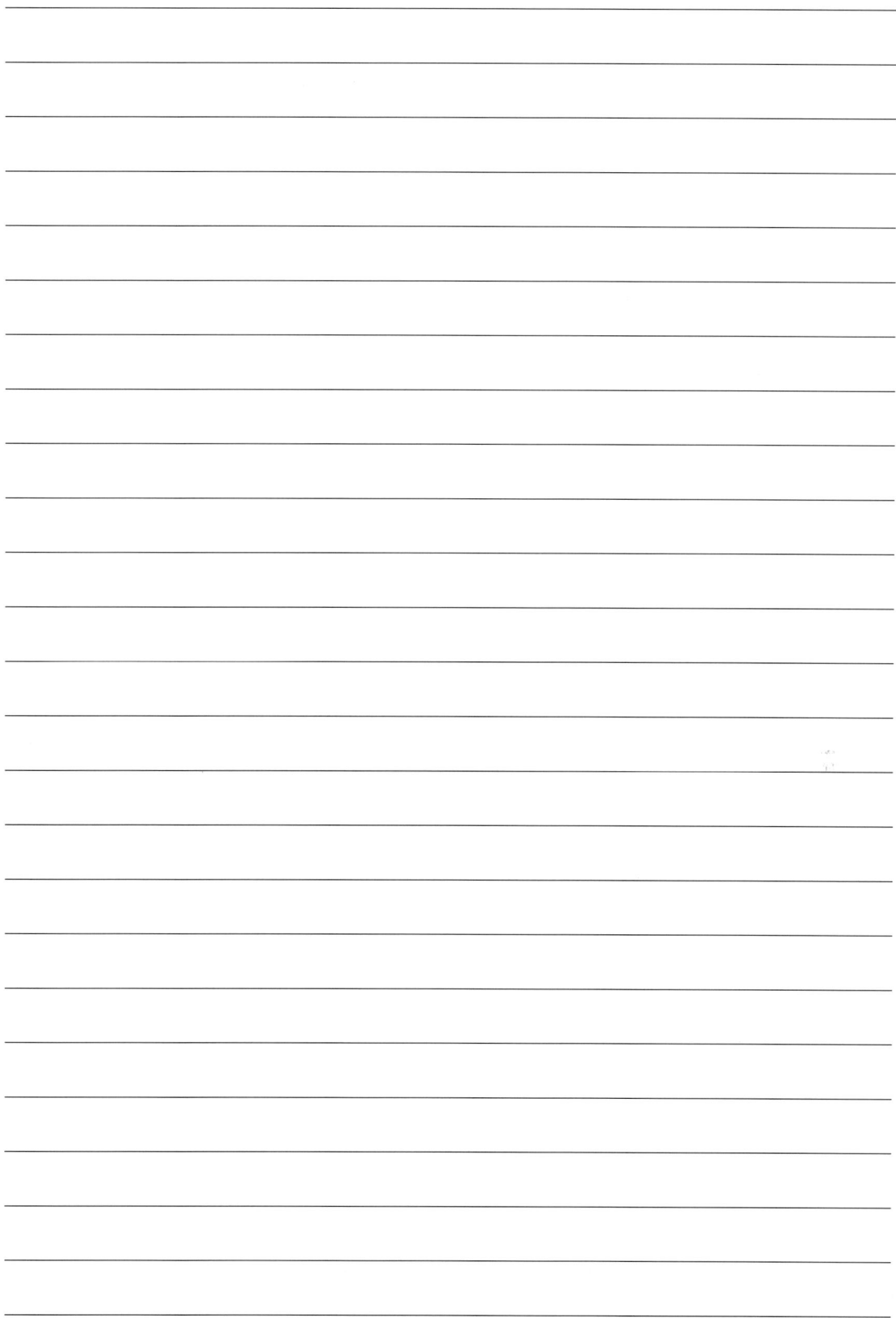

Date:	Anxiety Scale (1-10): AM PM
Today was I compassionate with myself or critical?	Are my thoughts giving me power or taking it away?

Are my thoughts true? *Really true?*

Am I avoiding something that I need to deal with?

Am I forecasting the future?

Am I "catastrophizing"?

Did I experience fear today?	Did it actually come true?
What helps to ease my anxiety?	Did I remember that?
Did I nourish my body and drink enough water?	Did I get fresh air?
How did I move my body today?	Did I try to practice mindfulness and deep breathing?
Did I have "What if's" today?	I am grateful for:

Promise me you'll always remember:
You're braver than you believe, stronger than you seem and smarter than you think.
A.A. Milne

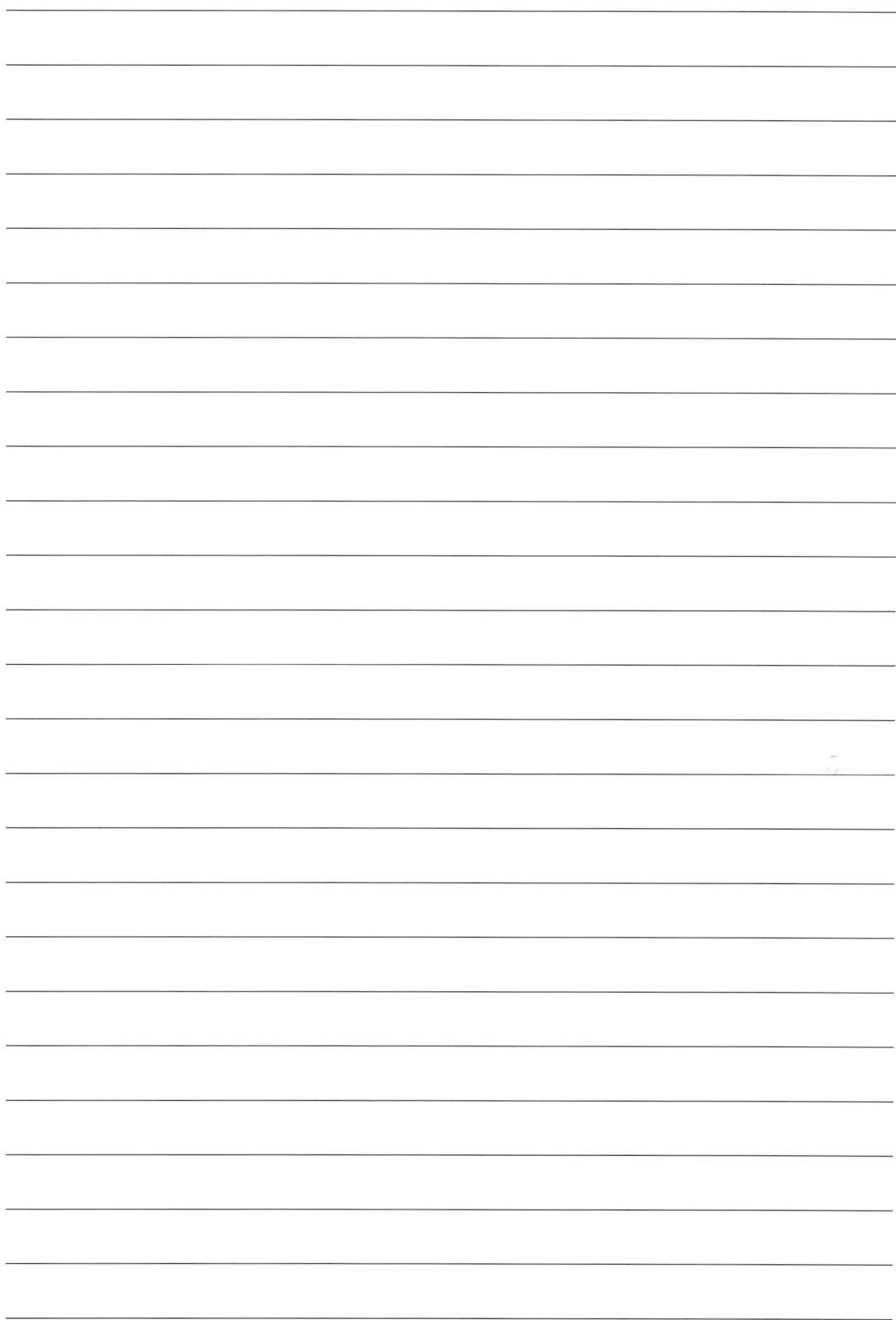

REVIEW OF LAST WEEK

Overall my week was…

Did I have the support I needed?

Did I ask for help when I needed it?

Did I remember my intentions from last week?

Did I spend enough time being unplugged?

I am proud that I….

Notes:

WEEKLY CHECK-IN

My Intention for Next Week:

I would like to:

Experience...

Let go of...

Feel...

Learn to...

Stop...

I want more...	I want less...

Date:	Anxiety Scale (1-10): AM PM
Today was I compassionate with myself or critical?	Are my thoughts giving me power or taking it away?

Are my thoughts true? *Really true?*

Am I avoiding something that I need to deal with?

Am I forecasting the future?

Am I "catastrophizing"?

Did I experience fear today?	Did it actually come true?
What helps to ease my anxiety?	Did I remember that?
Did I nourish my body and drink enough water?	Did I get fresh air?
How did I move my body today?	Did I try to practice mindfulness and deep breathing?
Did I have "What if's" today?	I am grateful for:

Promise me you'll always remember:
You're braver than you believe, stronger than you seem and smarter than you think.
A.A. Milne

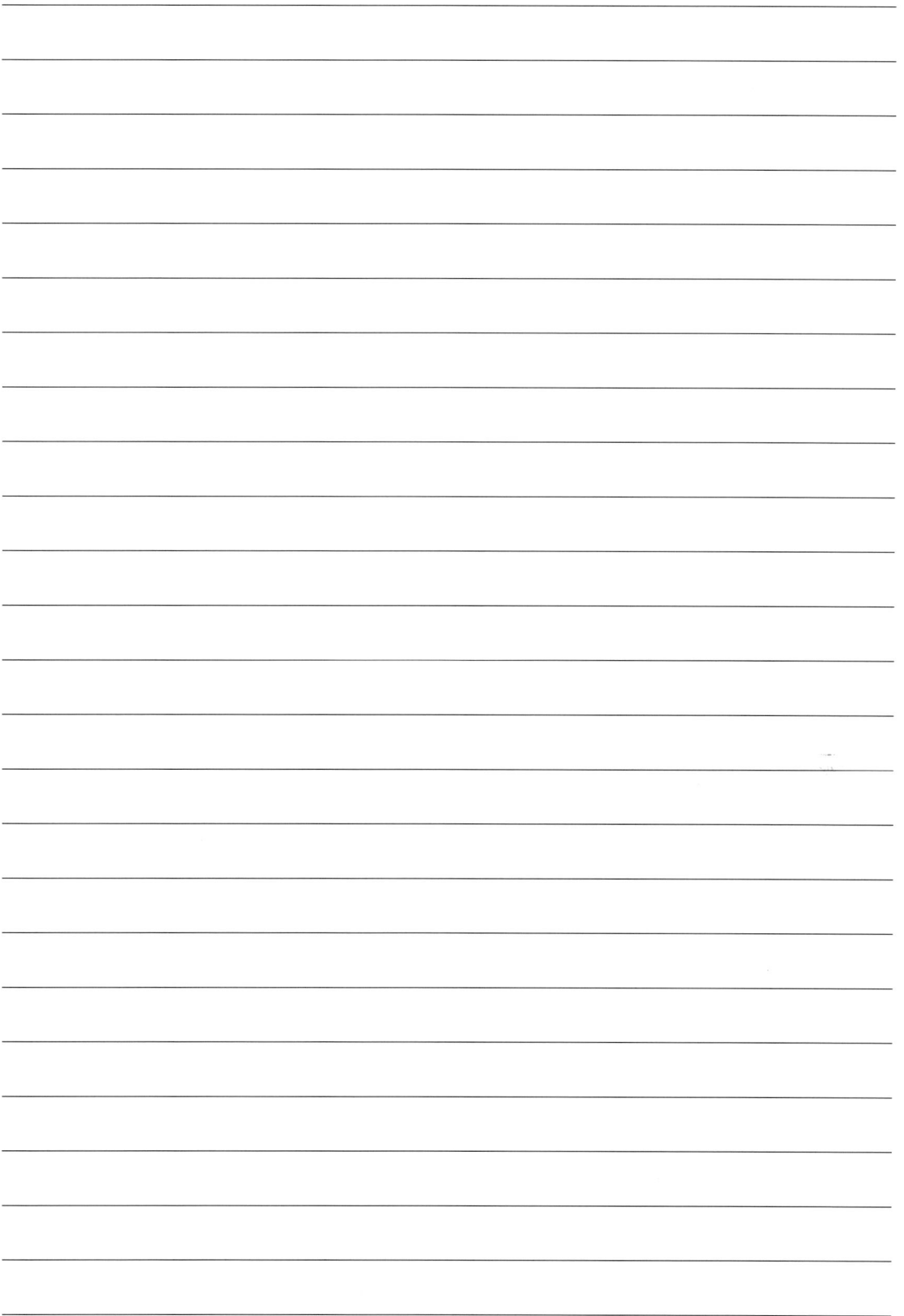

Date:	Anxiety Scale (1-10): AM PM
Today was I compassionate with myself or critical?	Are my thoughts giving me power or taking it away?
Are my thoughts true? *Really true?*	
Am I avoiding something that I need to deal with?	
Am I forecasting the future?	
Am I "catastrophizing"?	

Did I experience fear today?	Did it actually come true?
What helps to ease my anxiety?	Did I remember that?
Did I nourish my body and drink enough water?	Did I get fresh air?
How did I move my body today?	Did I try to practice mindfulness and deep breathing?
Did I have "What if's" today?	I am grateful for:

Promise me you'll always remember:
You're braver than you believe, stronger than you seem and smarter than you think.
A.A. Milne

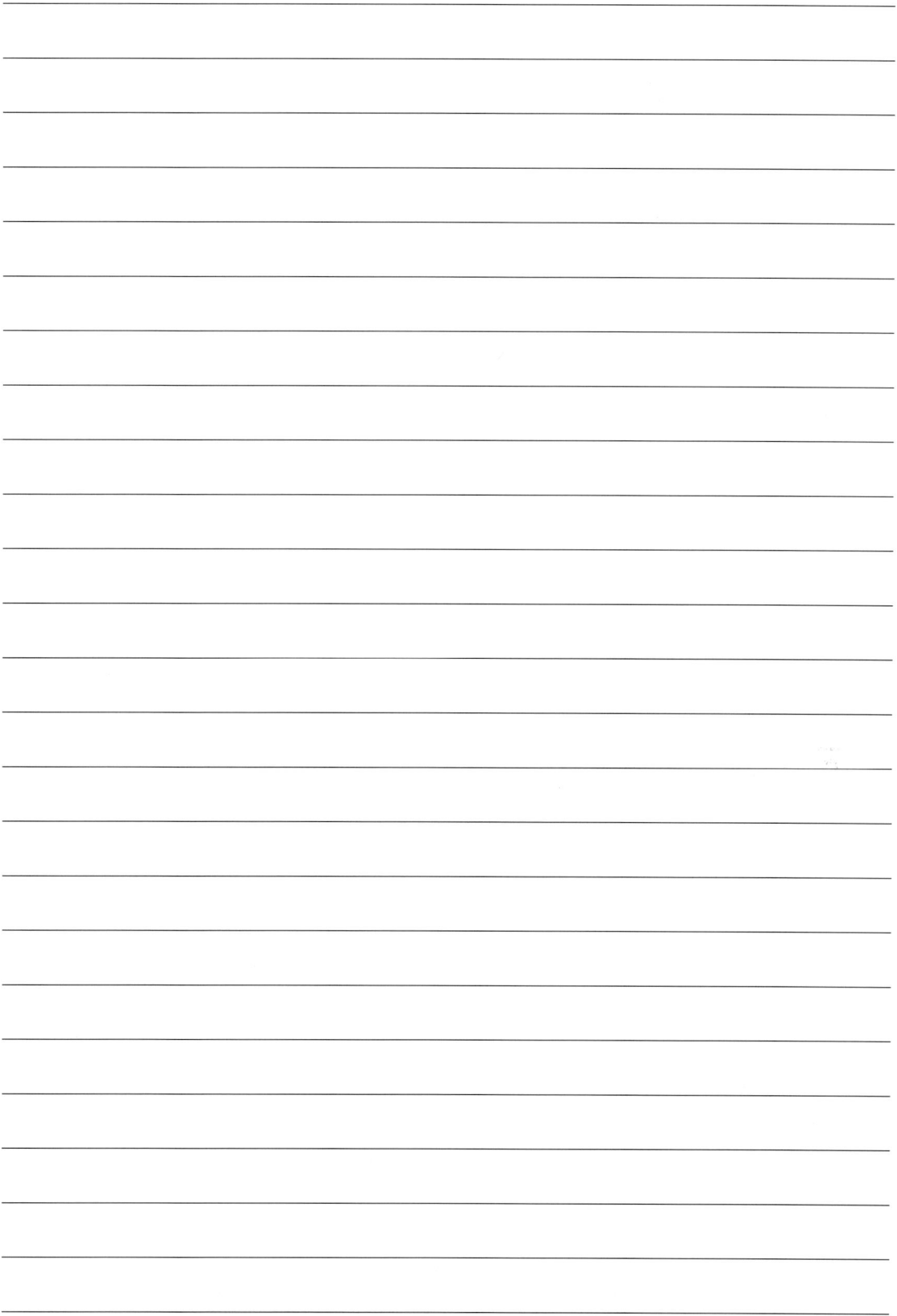

Date:	Anxiety Scale (1-10): AM PM
Today was I compassionate with myself or critical?	Are my thoughts giving me power or taking it away?

Are my thoughts true? *Really true?*

Am I avoiding something that I need to deal with?

Am I forecasting the future?

Am I "catastrophizing"?

Did I experience fear today?	Did it actually come true?
What helps to ease my anxiety?	Did I remember that?
Did I nourish my body and drink enough water?	Did I get fresh air?
How did I move my body today?	Did I try to practice mindfulness and deep breathing?
Did I have "What if's" today?	I am grateful for:

Promise me you'll always remember:
You're braver than you believe, stronger than you seem and smarter than you think.
A.A. Milne

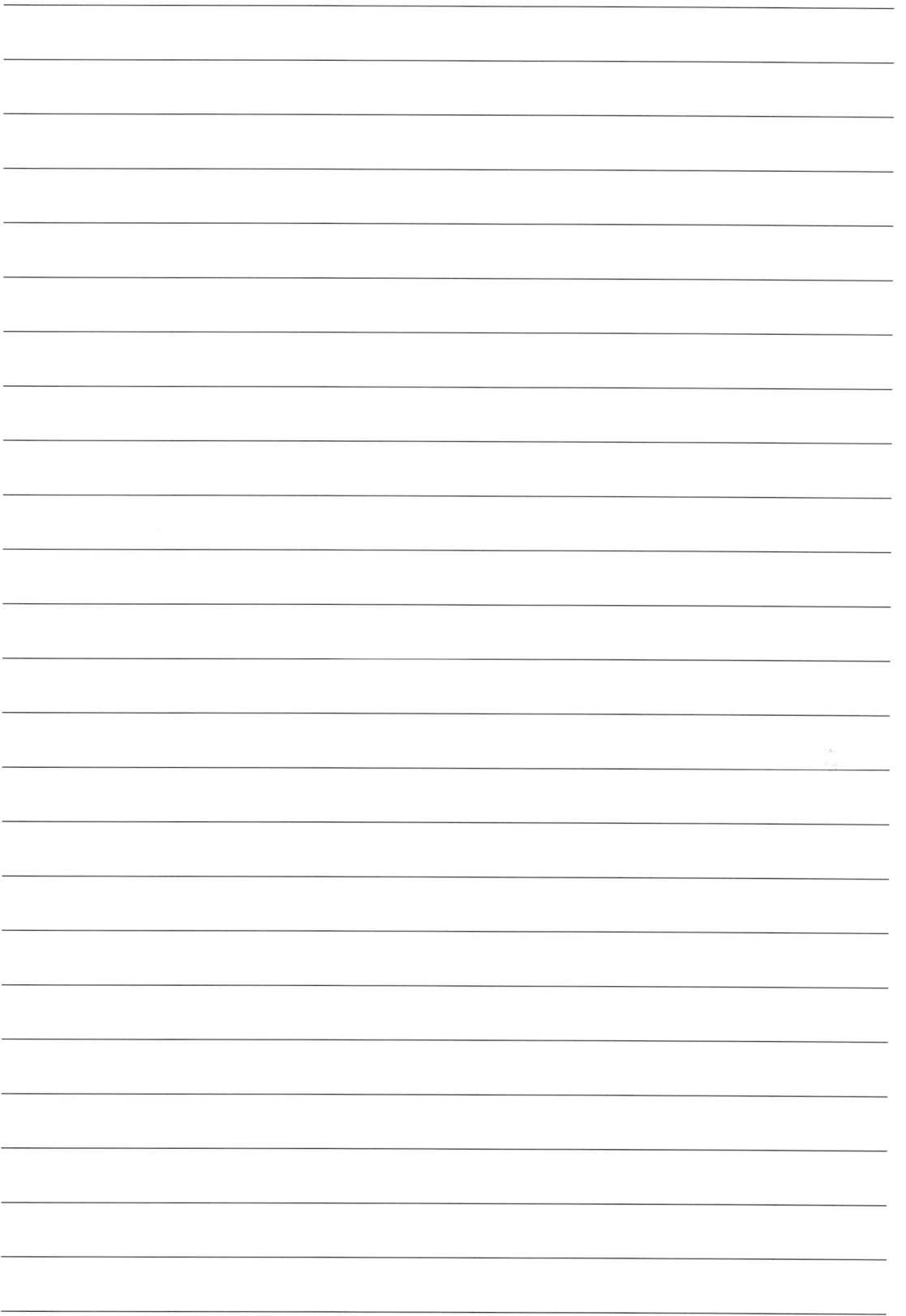

Date:	Anxiety Scale (1-10): AM PM
Today was I compassionate with myself or critical?	Are my thoughts giving me power or taking it away?

Are my thoughts true? *Really true?*

Am I avoiding something that I need to deal with?

Am I forecasting the future?

Am I "catastrophizing"?

Did I experience fear today?	Did it actually come true?
What helps to ease my anxiety?	Did I remember that?
Did I nourish my body and drink enough water?	Did I get fresh air?
How did I move my body today?	Did I try to practice mindfulness and deep breathing?
Did I have "What if's" today?	I am grateful for:

Promise me you'll always remember:
You're braver than you believe, stronger than you seem and smarter than you think.
A.A. Milne

Date:	Anxiety Scale (1-10): AM PM
Today was I compassionate with myself or critical?	Are my thoughts giving me power or taking it away?

Are my thoughts true? *Really true?*

Am I avoiding something that I need to deal with?

Am I forecasting the future?

Am I "catastrophizing"?

Did I experience fear today?	Did it actually come true?
What helps to ease my anxiety?	Did I remember that?
Did I nourish my body and drink enough water?	Did I get fresh air?
How did I move my body today?	Did I try to practice mindfulness and deep breathing?
Did I have "What if's" today?	I am grateful for:

Promise me you'll always remember:
You're braver than you believe, stronger than you seem and smarter than you think.
A.A. Milne

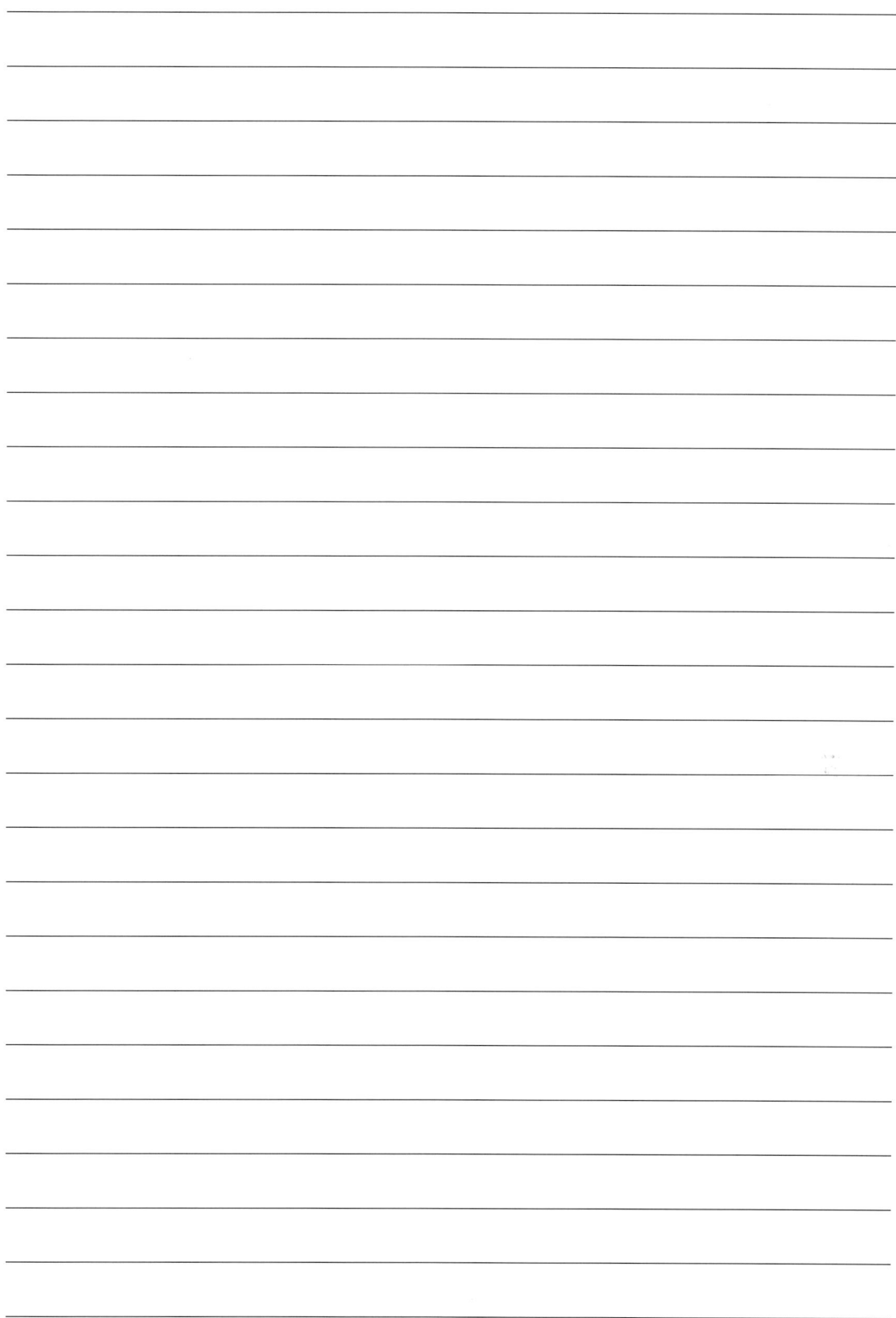

Date:	Anxiety Scale (1-10): AM PM
Today was I compassionate with myself or critical?	Are my thoughts giving me power or taking it away?

Are my thoughts true? *Really true?*

Am I avoiding something that I need to deal with?

Am I forecasting the future?

Am I "catastrophizing"?

Did I experience fear today?	Did it actually come true?
What helps to ease my anxiety?	Did I remember that?
Did I nourish my body and drink enough water?	Did I get fresh air?
How did I move my body today?	Did I try to practice mindfulness and deep breathing?
Did I have "What if's" today?	I am grateful for:

Promise me you'll always remember: You're braver than you believe, stronger than you seem and smarter than you think. *A.A. Milne*

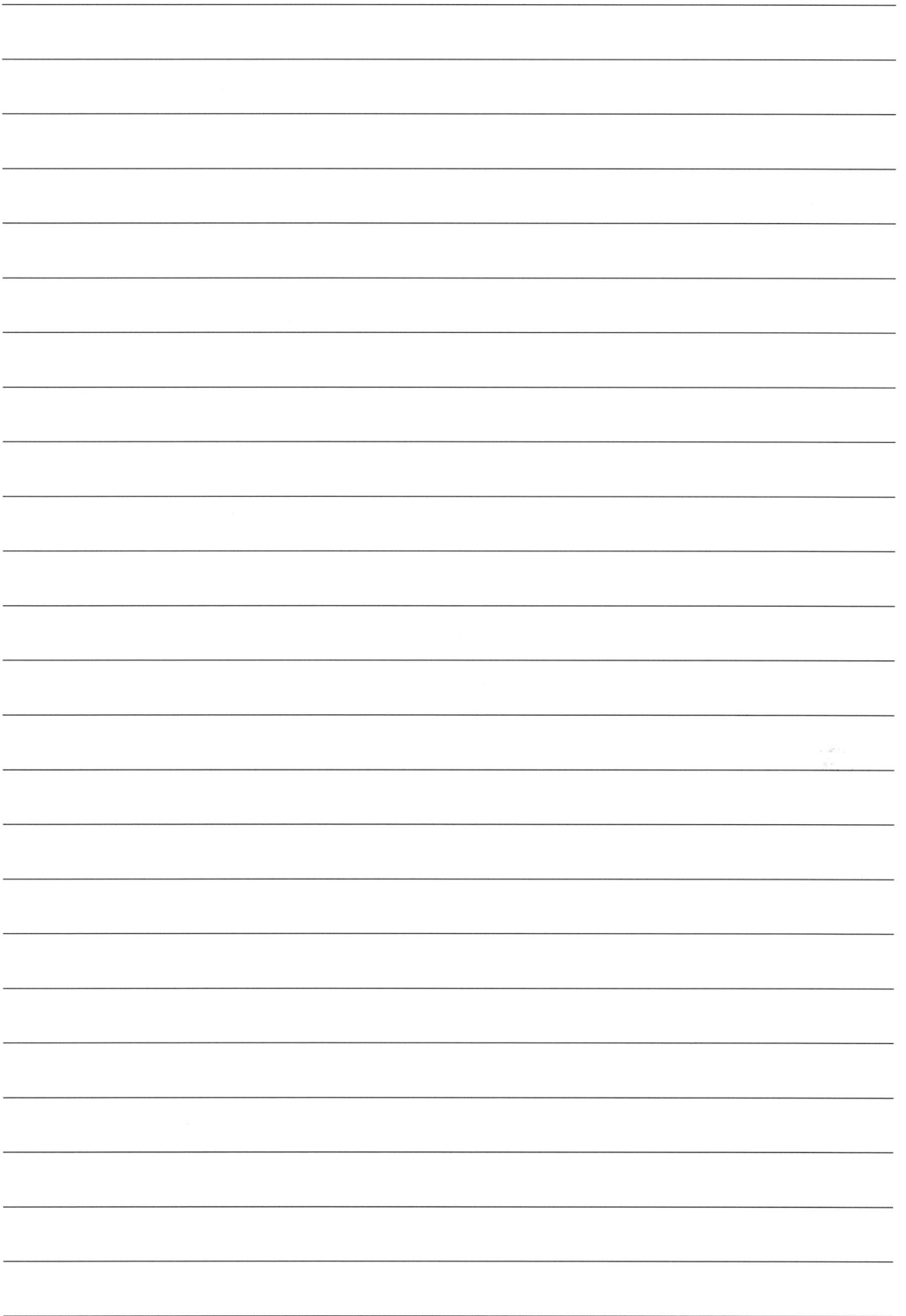

Date:	Anxiety Scale (1-10): AM PM
Today was I compassionate with myself or critical?	Are my thoughts giving me power or taking it away?
Are my thoughts true? *Really true?*	
Am I avoiding something that I need to deal with?	
Am I forecasting the future?	
Am I "catastrophizing"?	
Did I experience fear today?	Did it actually come true?
What helps to ease my anxiety?	Did I remember that?
Did I nourish my body and drink enough water?	Did I get fresh air?
How did I move my body today?	Did I try to practice mindfulness and deep breathing?
Did I have "What if's" today?	I am grateful for:

Promise me you'll always remember:
You're braver than you believe, stronger than you seem and smarter than you think.
A.A. Milne

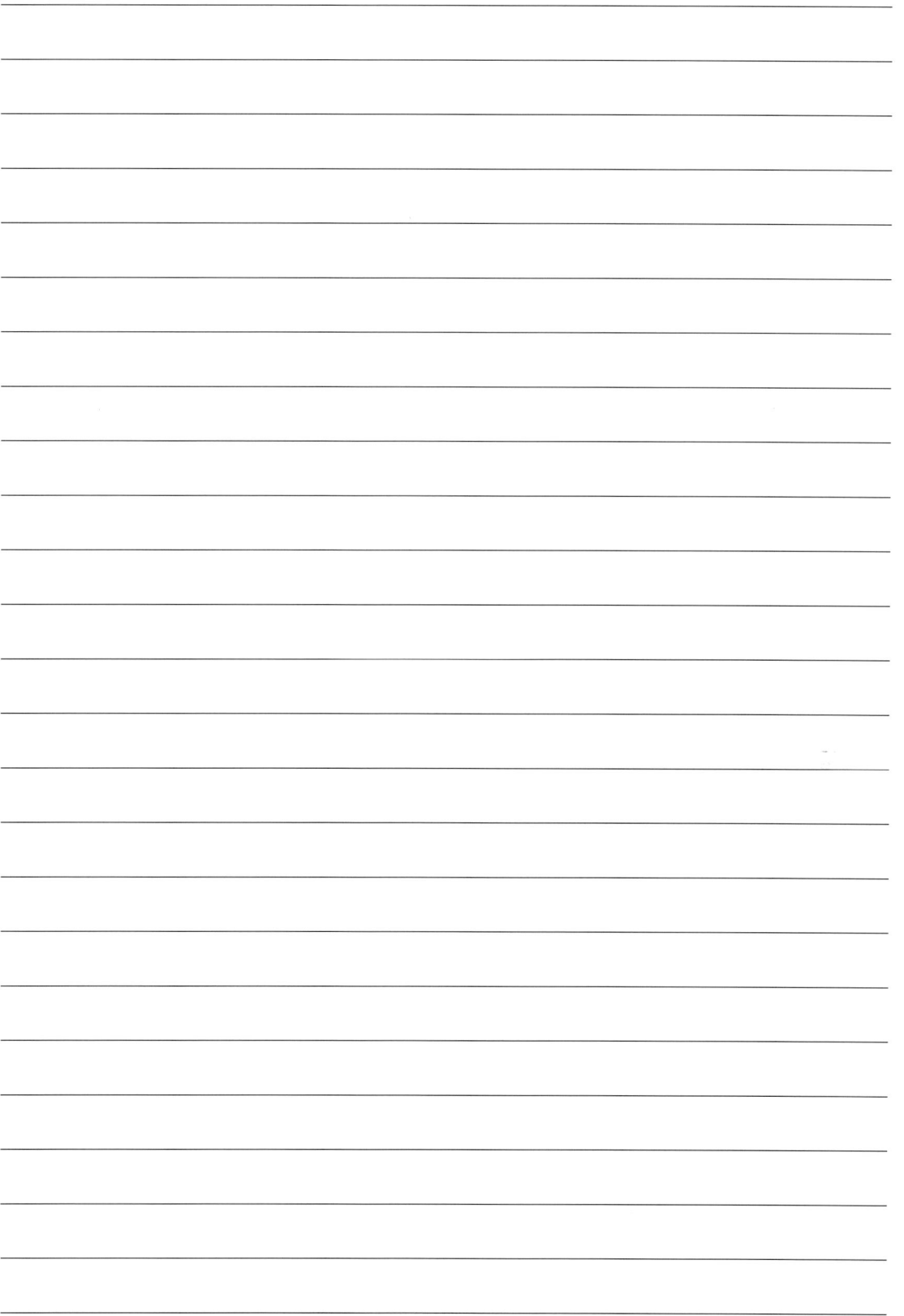

REVIEW OF LAST WEEK

Overall my week was...

Did I have the support I needed?

Did I ask for help when I needed it?

Did I remember my intentions from last week?

Did I spend enough time being unplugged?

I am proud that I....

Notes:

WEEKLY CHECK-IN

My Intention for Next Week:

I would like to:

Experience...

Let go of...

Feel...

Learn to...

Stop...

I want more...	I want less...

Date:	Anxiety Scale (1-10): AM PM
Today was I compassionate with myself or critical?	Are my thoughts giving me power or taking it away?

Are my thoughts true? *Really true?*

Am I avoiding something that I need to deal with?

Am I forecasting the future?

Am I "catastrophizing"?

Did I experience fear today?	Did it actually come true?
What helps to ease my anxiety?	Did I remember that?
Did I nourish my body and drink enough water?	Did I get fresh air?
How did I move my body today?	Did I try to practice mindfulness and deep breathing?
Did I have "What if's" today?	I am grateful for:

Promise me you'll always remember:
You're braver than you believe, stronger than you seem and smarter than you think.
A.A. Milne

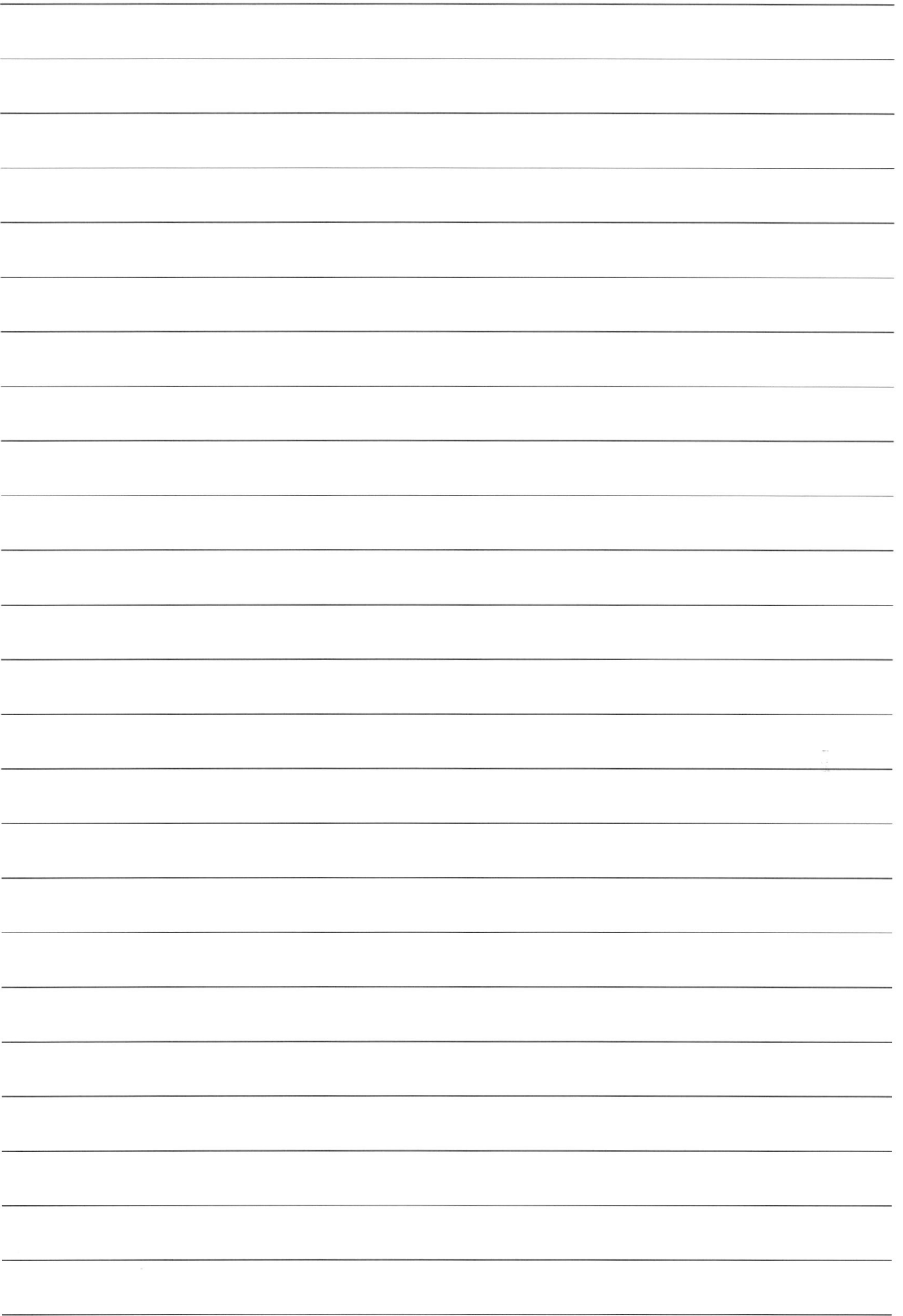

Date:	Anxiety Scale (1-10): AM PM
Today was I compassionate with myself or critical?	Are my thoughts giving me power or taking it away?

Are my thoughts true? *Really true?*

Am I avoiding something that I need to deal with?

Am I forecasting the future?

Am I "catastrophizing"?

Did I experience fear today?	Did it actually come true?
What helps to ease my anxiety?	Did I remember that?
Did I nourish my body and drink enough water?	Did I get fresh air?
How did I move my body today?	Did I try to practice mindfulness and deep breathing?
Did I have "What if's" today?	I am grateful for:

Promise me you'll always remember:
You're braver than you believe, stronger than you seem and smarter than you think.
A.A. Milne

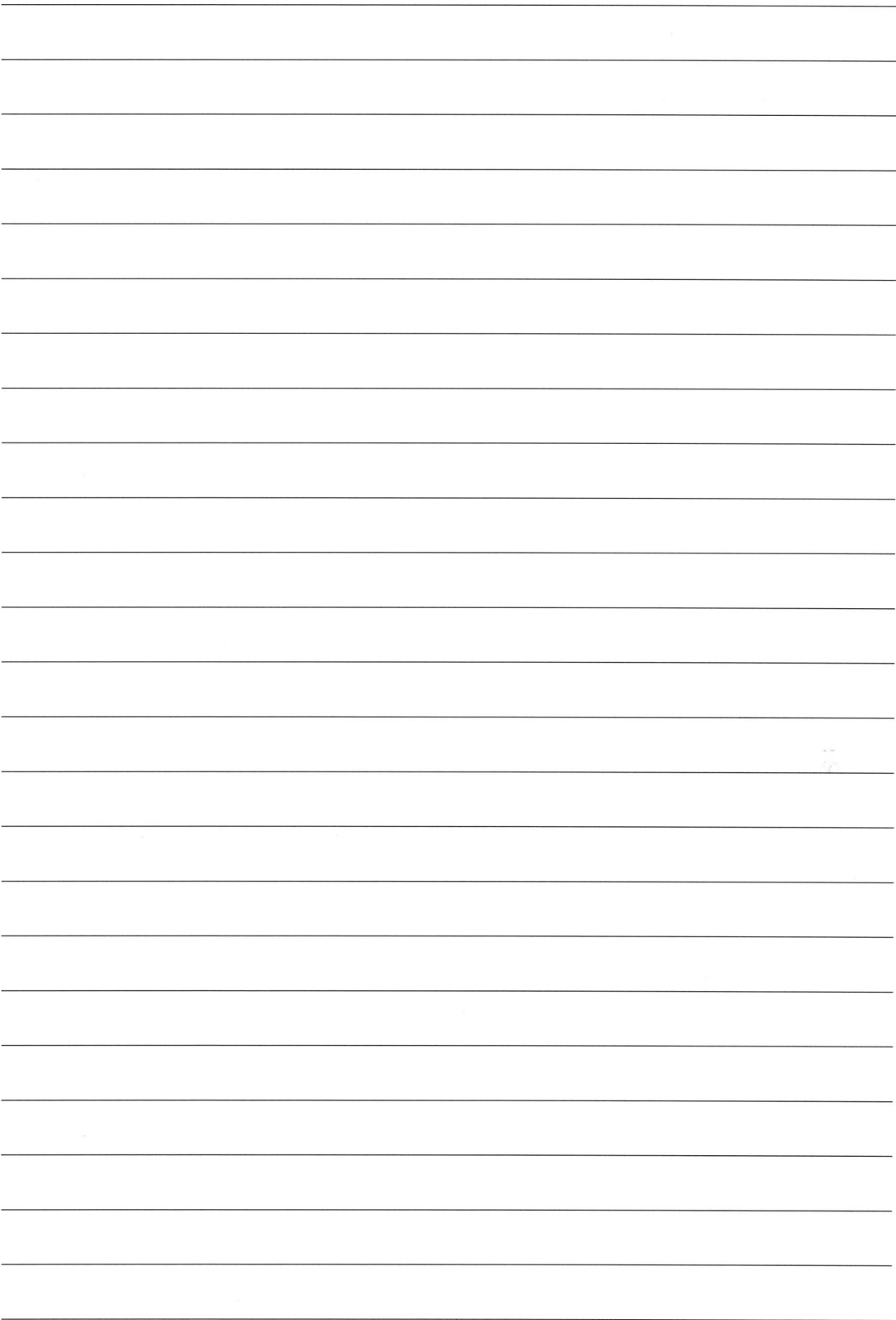

Date:	Anxiety Scale (1-10): AM PM
Today was I compassionate with myself or critical?	Are my thoughts giving me power or taking it away?

Are my thoughts true? *Really true?*

Am I avoiding something that I need to deal with?

Am I forecasting the future?

Am I "catastrophizing"?

Did I experience fear today?	Did it actually come true?
What helps to ease my anxiety?	Did I remember that?
Did I nourish my body and drink enough water?	Did I get fresh air?
How did I move my body today?	Did I try to practice mindfulness and deep breathing?
Did I have "What if's" today?	I am grateful for:

Promise me you'll always remember:
You're braver than you believe, stronger than you seem and smarter than you think.
A.A. Milne

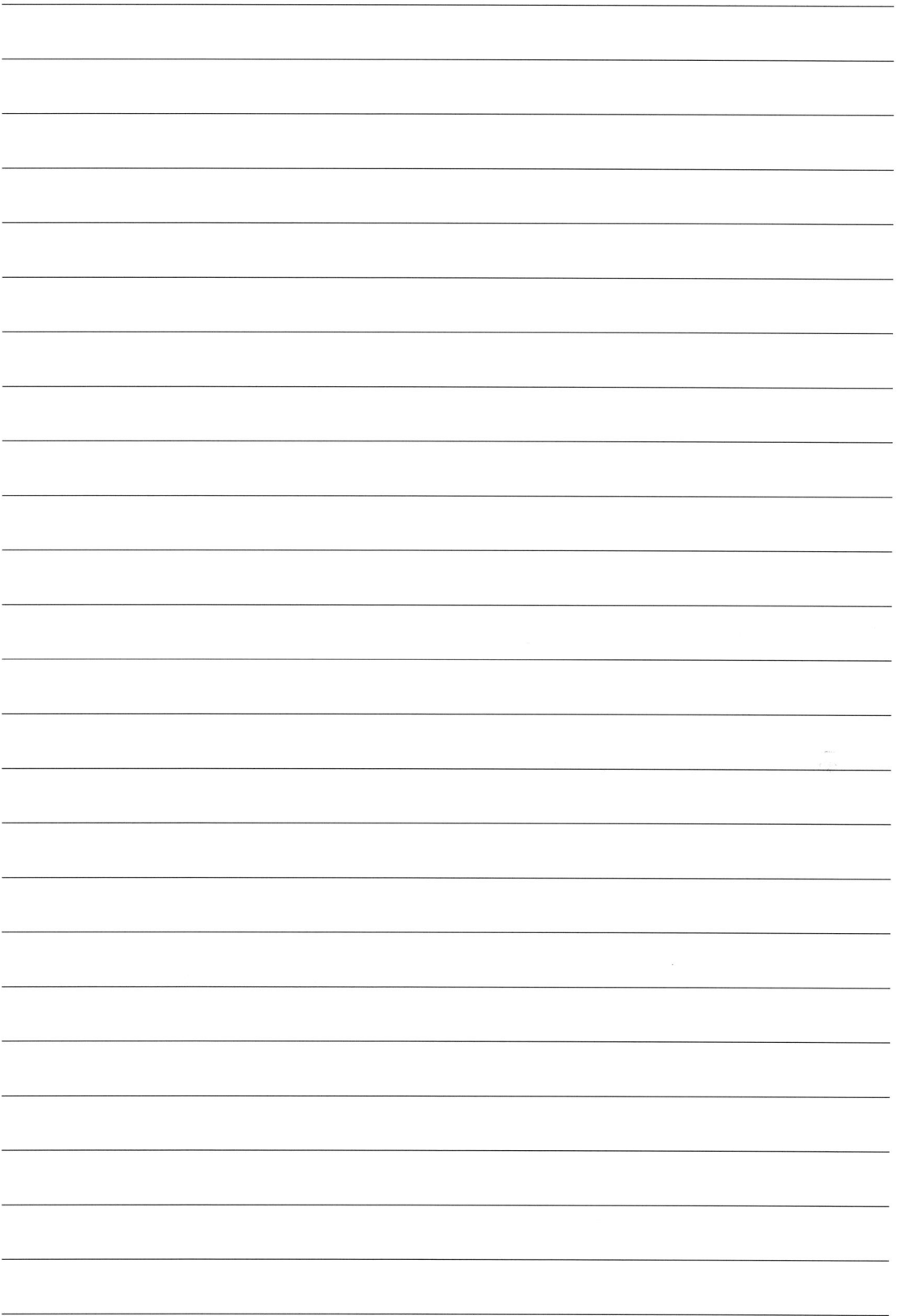

Date:	Anxiety Scale (1-10):
	AM PM

Today was I compassionate with myself or critical?	Are my thoughts giving me power or taking it away?

Are my thoughts true? *Really true?*

Am I avoiding something that I need to deal with?

Am I forecasting the future?

Am I "catastrophizing"?

Did I experience fear today?	Did it actually come true?

What helps to ease my anxiety?	Did I remember that?

Did I nourish my body and drink enough water?	Did I get fresh air?

How did I move my body today?	Did I try to practice mindfulness and deep breathing?

Did I have "What if's" today?	I am grateful for:

Promise me you'll always remember:
You're braver than you believe, stronger than you seem and smarter than you think.
A.A. Milne

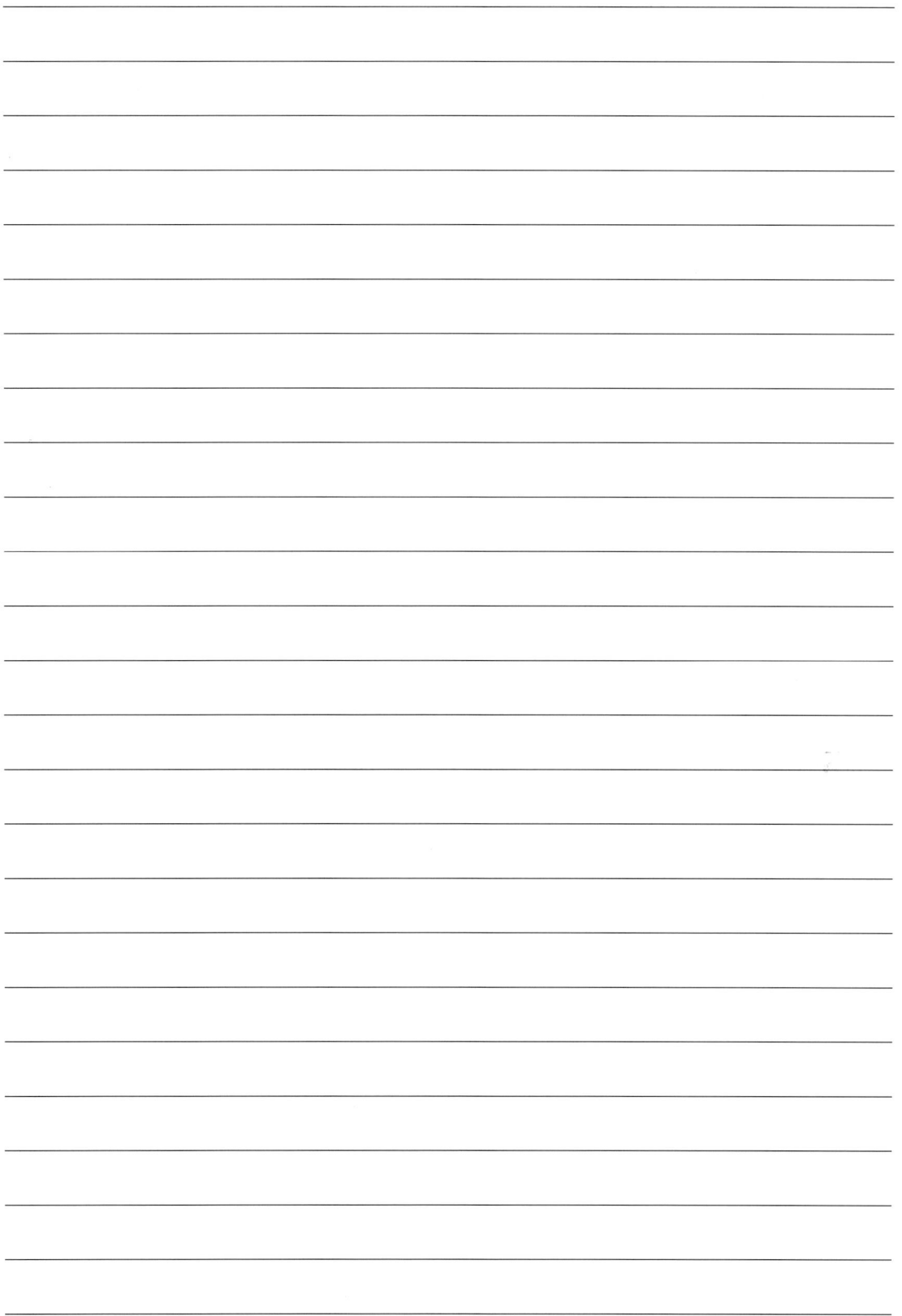

Date:	Anxiety Scale (1-10): AM PM
Today was I compassionate with myself or critical?	Are my thoughts giving me power or taking it away?

Are my thoughts true? *Really true?*

Am I avoiding something that I need to deal with?

Am I forecasting the future?

Am I "catastrophizing"?

Did I experience fear today?	Did it actually come true?
What helps to ease my anxiety?	Did I remember that?
Did I nourish my body and drink enough water?	Did I get fresh air?
How did I move my body today?	Did I try to practice mindfulness and deep breathing?
Did I have "What if's" today?	I am grateful for:

Promise me you'll always remember:
You're braver than you believe, stronger than you seem and smarter than you think.
A.A. Milne

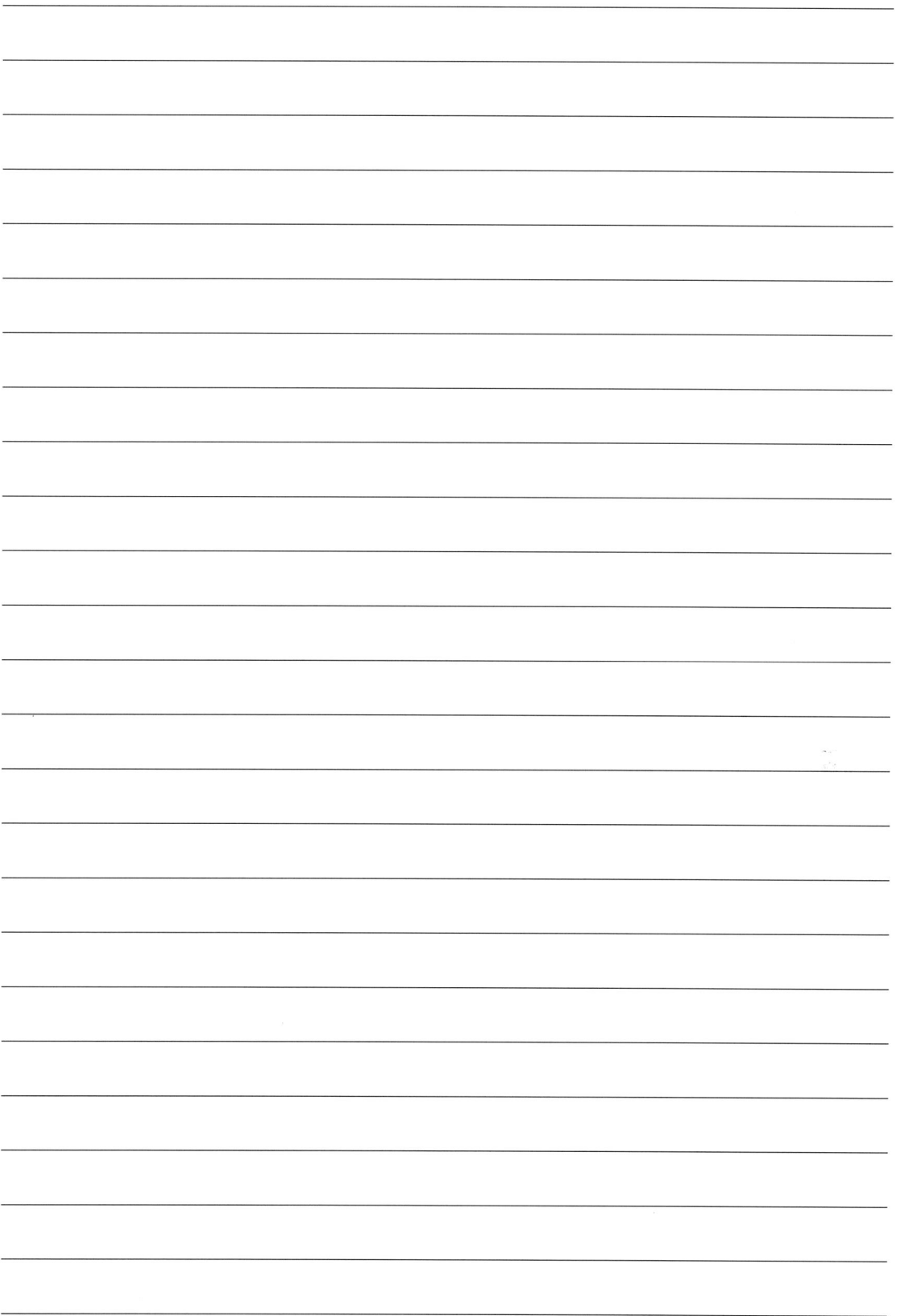

Date:	Anxiety Scale (1-10): AM PM
Today was I compassionate with myself or critical?	Are my thoughts giving me power or taking it away?

Are my thoughts true? *Really true?*

Am I avoiding something that I need to deal with?

Am I forecasting the future?

Am I "catastrophizing"?

Did I experience fear today?	Did it actually come true?
What helps to ease my anxiety?	Did I remember that?
Did I nourish my body and drink enough water?	Did I get fresh air?
How did I move my body today?	Did I try to practice mindfulness and deep breathing?
Did I have "What if's" today?	I am grateful for:

Promise me you'll always remember:
You're braver than you believe, stronger than you seem and smarter than you think.
A.A. Milne

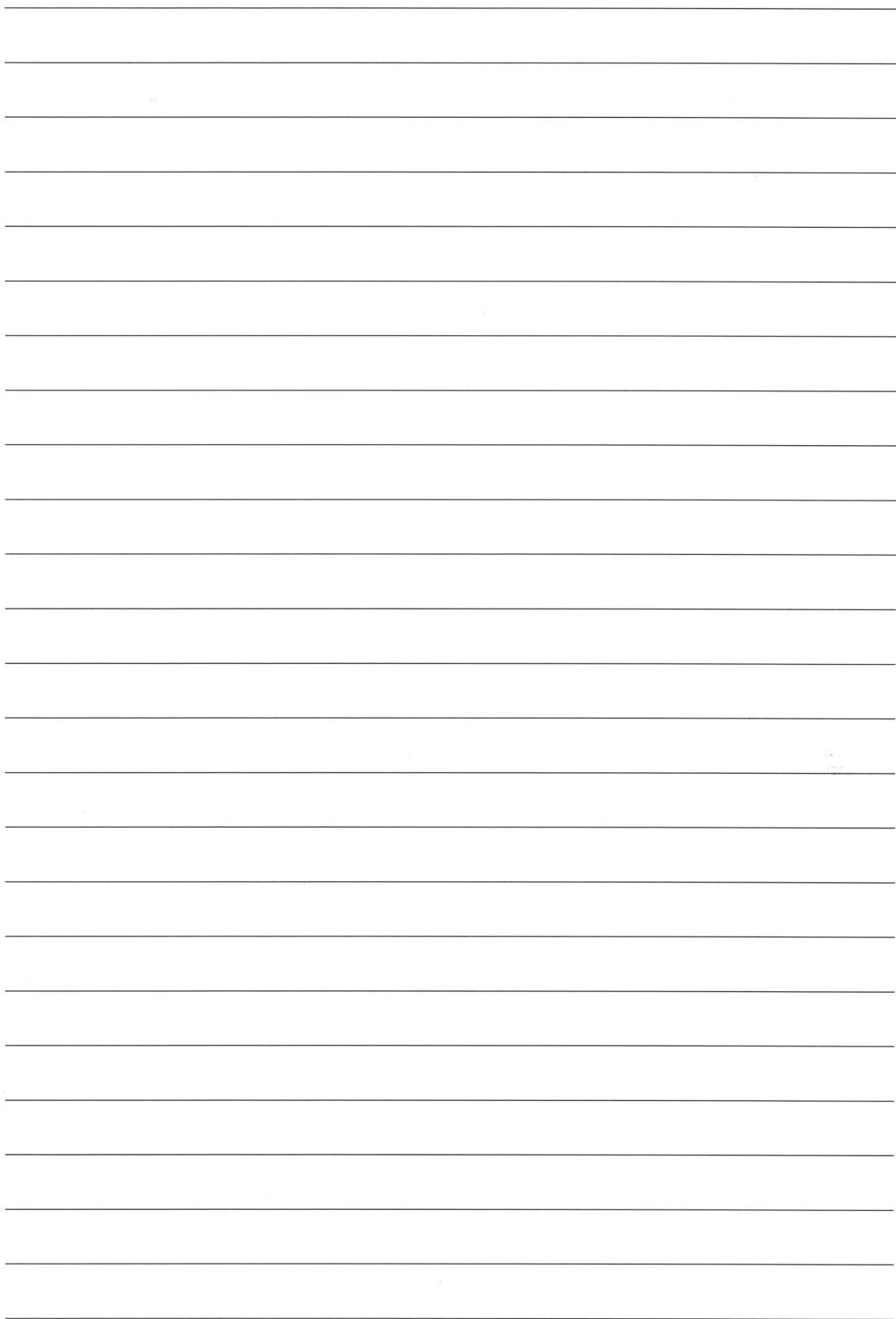

Date:	Anxiety Scale (1-10): AM PM
Today was I compassionate with myself or critical?	Are my thoughts giving me power or taking it away?

Are my thoughts true? *Really true?*

Am I avoiding something that I need to deal with?

Am I forecasting the future?

Am I "catastrophizing"?

Did I experience fear today?	Did it actually come true?
What helps to ease my anxiety?	Did I remember that?
Did I nourish my body and drink enough water?	Did I get fresh air?
How did I move my body today?	Did I try to practice mindfulness and deep breathing?
Did I have "What if's" today?	I am grateful for:

Promise me you'll always remember:
You're braver than you believe, stronger than you seem and smarter than you think.
A.A. Milne

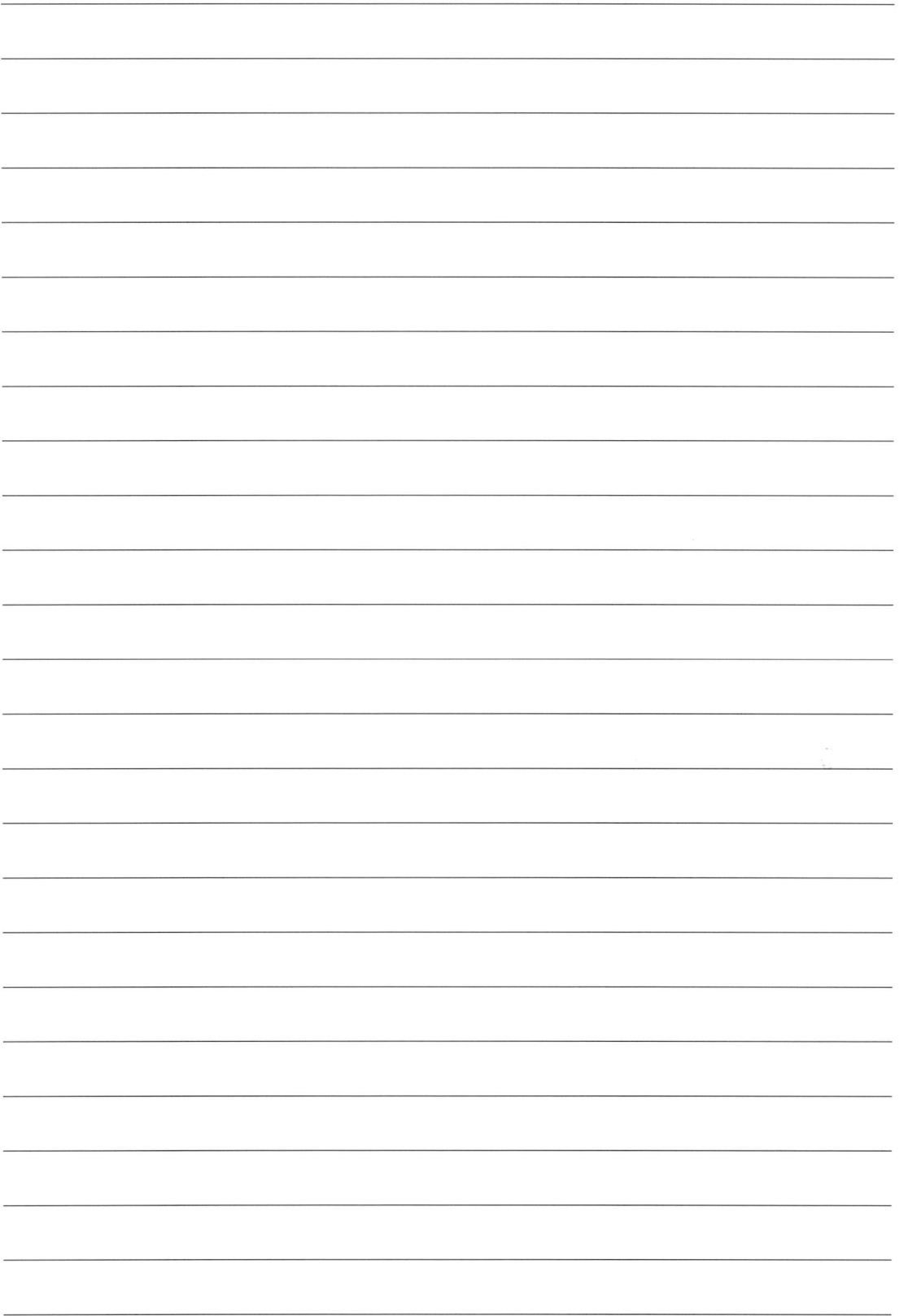

REVIEW OF LAST WEEK

Overall my week was...

Did I have the support I needed?	Did I ask for help when I needed it?

Did I remember my intentions from last week?

Did I spend enough time being unplugged?

I am proud that I....

Notes:

WEEKLY CHECK-IN

My Intention for Next Week:

I would like to:

Experience...

Let go of...

Feel...

Learn to...

Stop...

I want more...	I want less...

Date:	Anxiety Scale (1-10): AM PM
Today was I compassionate with myself or critical?	Are my thoughts giving me power or taking it away?

Are my thoughts true? *Really true?*

Am I avoiding something that I need to deal with?

Am I forecasting the future?

Am I "catastrophizing"?

Did I experience fear today?	Did it actually come true?
What helps to ease my anxiety?	Did I remember that?
Did I nourish my body and drink enough water?	Did I get fresh air?
How did I move my body today?	Did I try to practice mindfulness and deep breathing?
Did I have "What if's" today?	I am grateful for:

Promise me you'll always remember:
You're braver than you believe, stronger than you seem and smarter than you think.
A.A. Milne

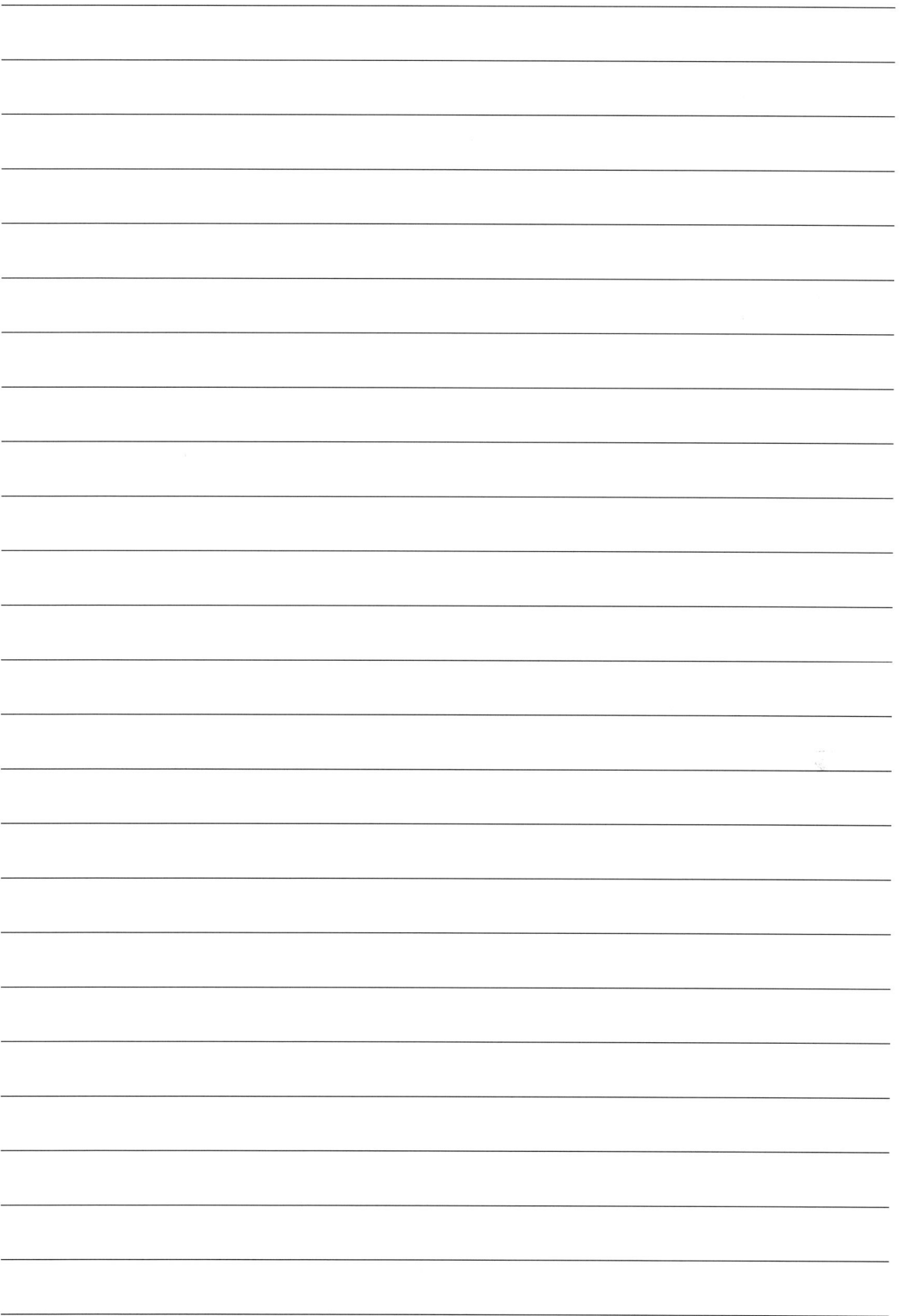

Date:	Anxiety Scale (1-10): AM PM
Today was I compassionate with myself or critical?	Are my thoughts giving me power or taking it away?

Are my thoughts true? *Really true?*

Am I avoiding something that I need to deal with?

Am I forecasting the future?

Am I "catastrophizing"?

Did I experience fear today?	Did it actually come true?
What helps to ease my anxiety?	Did I remember that?
Did I nourish my body and drink enough water?	Did I get fresh air?
How did I move my body today?	Did I try to practice mindfulness and deep breathing?
Did I have "What if's" today?	I am grateful for:

Promise me you'll always remember:
You're braver than you believe, stronger than you seem and smarter than you think.
A.A. Milne

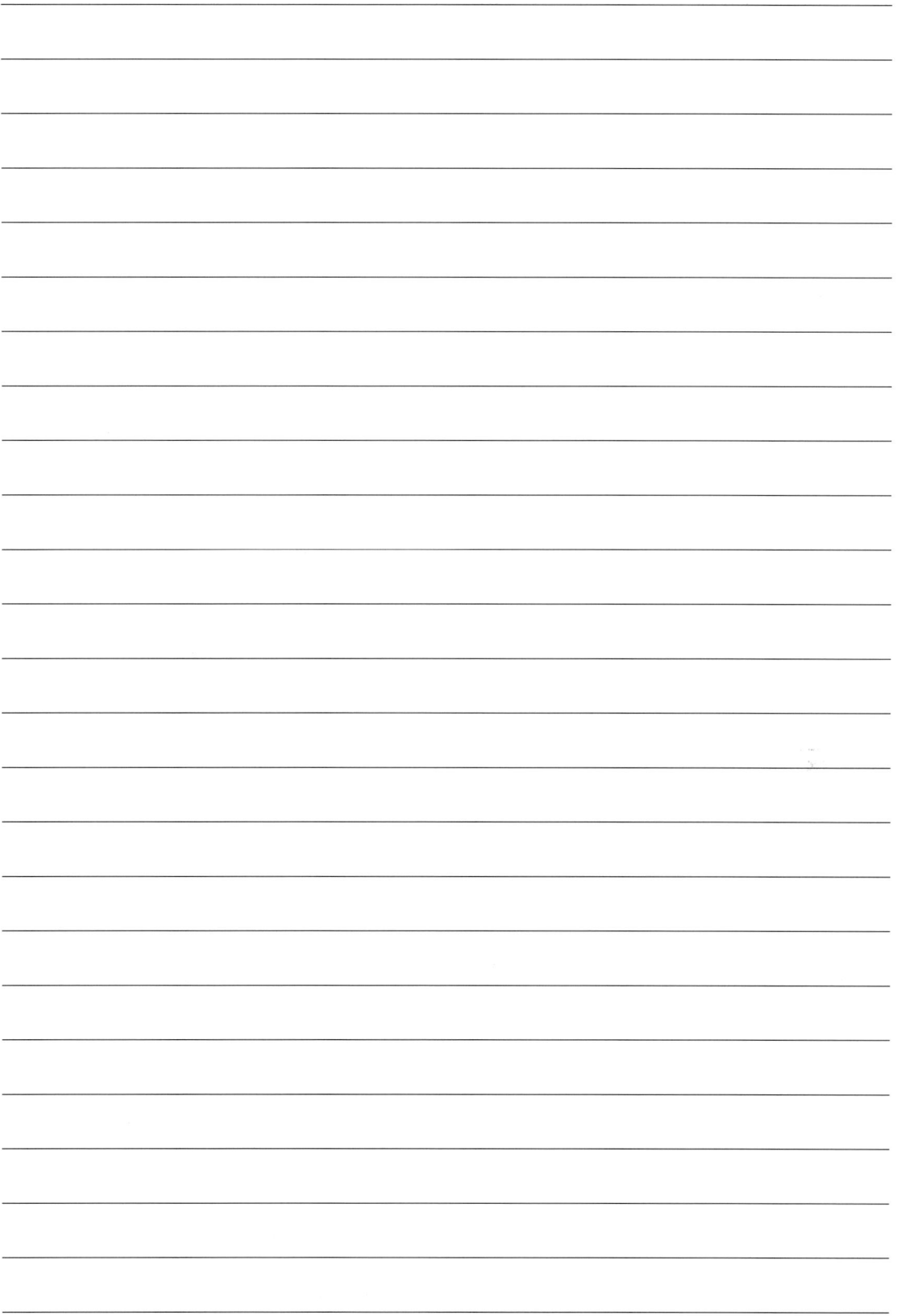

Date:	Anxiety Scale (1-10): AM PM
Today was I compassionate with myself or critical?	Are my thoughts giving me power or taking it away?

Are my thoughts true? *Really true?*

Am I avoiding something that I need to deal with?

Am I forecasting the future?

Am I "catastrophizing"?

Did I experience fear today?	Did it actually come true?
What helps to ease my anxiety?	Did I remember that?
Did I nourish my body and drink enough water?	Did I get fresh air?
How did I move my body today?	Did I try to practice mindfulness and deep breathing?
Did I have "What if's" today?	I am grateful for:

Promise me you'll always remember:
You're braver than you believe, stronger than you seem and smarter than you think.
A.A. Milne

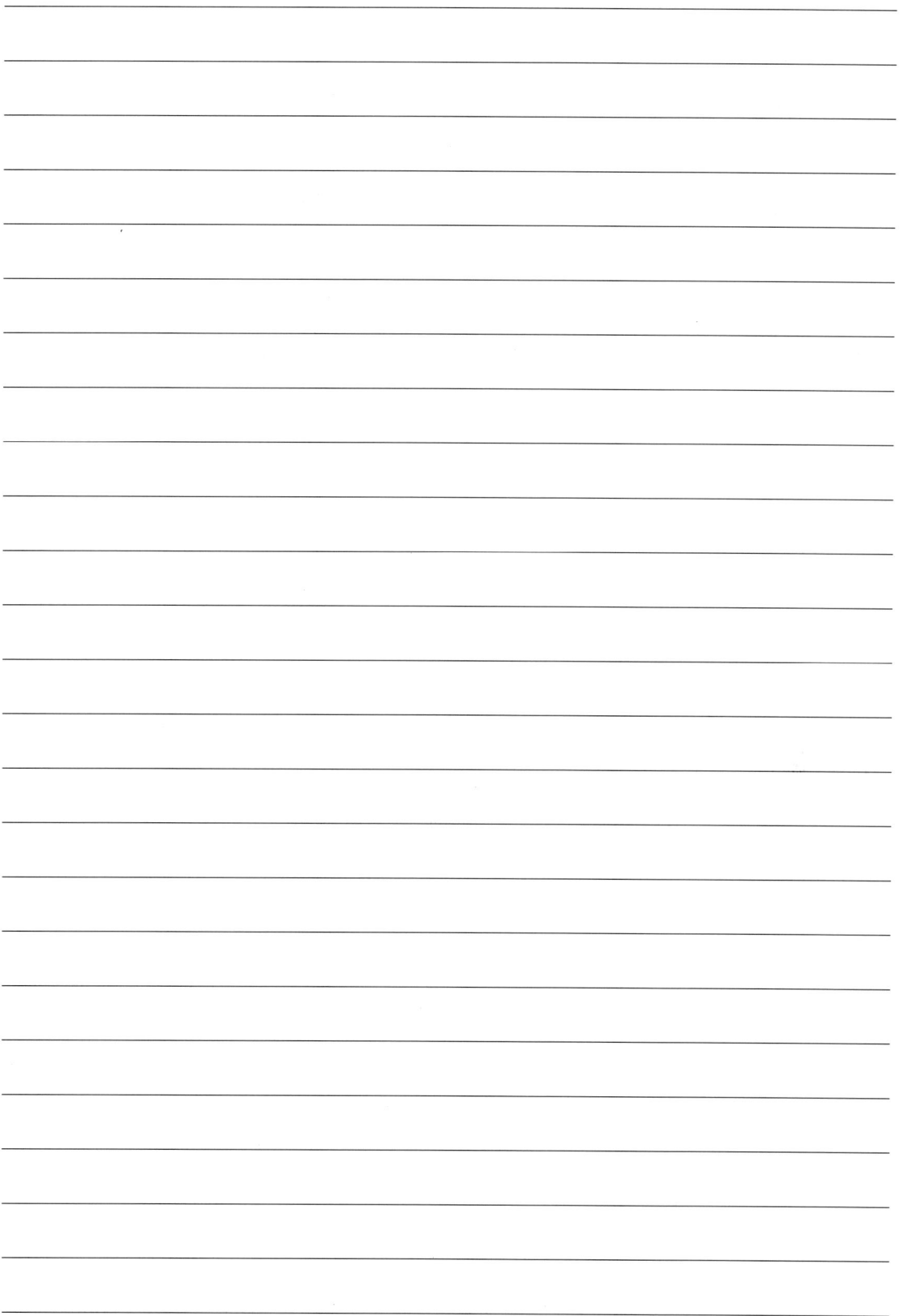

Date:	Anxiety Scale (1-10): AM PM
Today was I compassionate with myself or critical?	Are my thoughts giving me power or taking it away?

Are my thoughts true? *Really true?*

Am I avoiding something that I need to deal with?

Am I forecasting the future?

Am I "catastrophizing"?

Did I experience fear today?	Did it actually come true?
What helps to ease my anxiety?	Did I remember that?
Did I nourish my body and drink enough water?	Did I get fresh air?
How did I move my body today?	Did I try to practice mindfulness and deep breathing?
Did I have "What if's" today?	I am grateful for:

Promise me you'll always remember:
You're braver than you believe, stronger than you seem and smarter than you think.
A.A. Milne

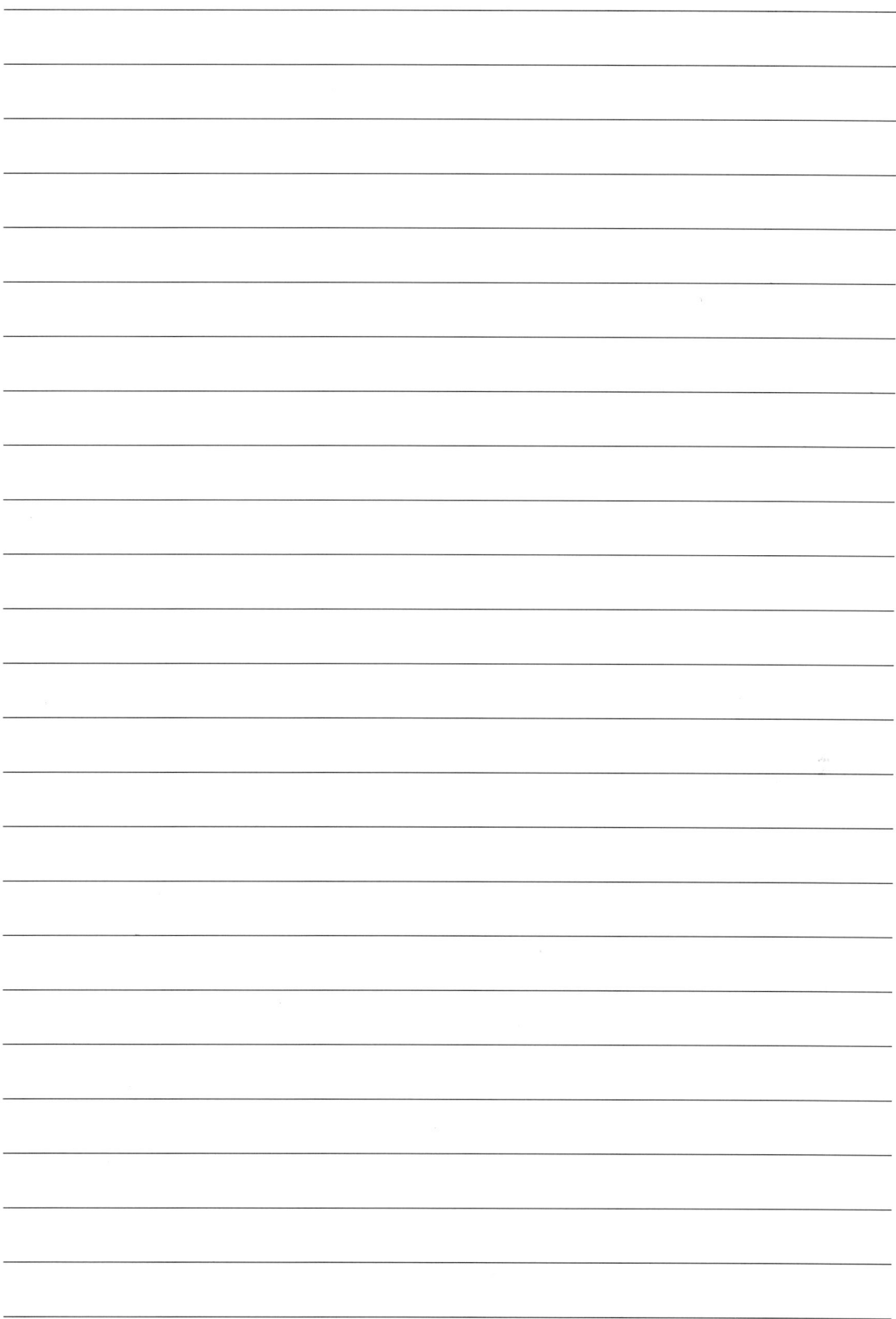

| Date: | Anxiety Scale (1-10): |
| | AM   PM |

| Today was I compassionate with myself or critical? | Are my thoughts giving me power or taking it away? |

Are my thoughts true? *Really true?*

Am I avoiding something that I need to deal with?

Am I forecasting the future?

Am I "catastrophizing"?

| Did I experience fear today? | Did it actually come true? |

| What helps to ease my anxiety? | Did I remember that? |

| Did I nourish my body and drink enough water? | Did I get fresh air? |

| How did I move my body today? | Did I try to practice mindfulness and deep breathing? |

| Did I have "What if's" today? | I am grateful for: |

Promise me you'll always remember:
You're braver than you believe, stronger than you seem and smarter than you think.
A.A. Milne

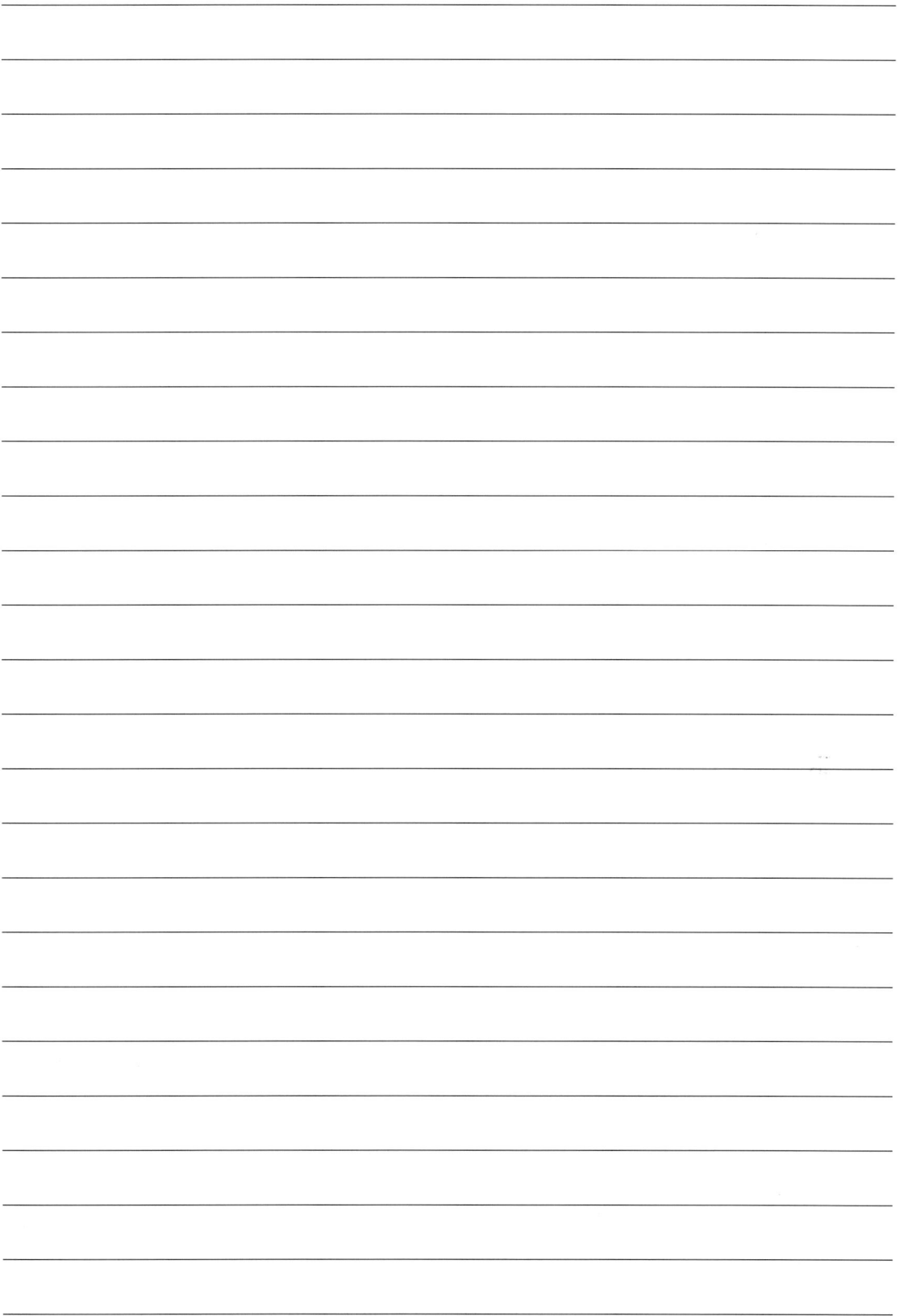

Date:	Anxiety Scale (1-10): AM PM
Today was I compassionate with myself or critical?	Are my thoughts giving me power or taking it away?

Are my thoughts true? *Really true?*

Am I avoiding something that I need to deal with?

Am I forecasting the future?

Am I "catastrophizing"?

Did I experience fear today?	Did it actually come true?
What helps to ease my anxiety?	Did I remember that?
Did I nourish my body and drink enough water?	Did I get fresh air?
How did I move my body today?	Did I try to practice mindfulness and deep breathing?
Did I have "What if's" today?	I am grateful for:

Promise me you'll always remember:
You're braver than you believe, stronger than you seem and smarter than you think.
A.A. Milne

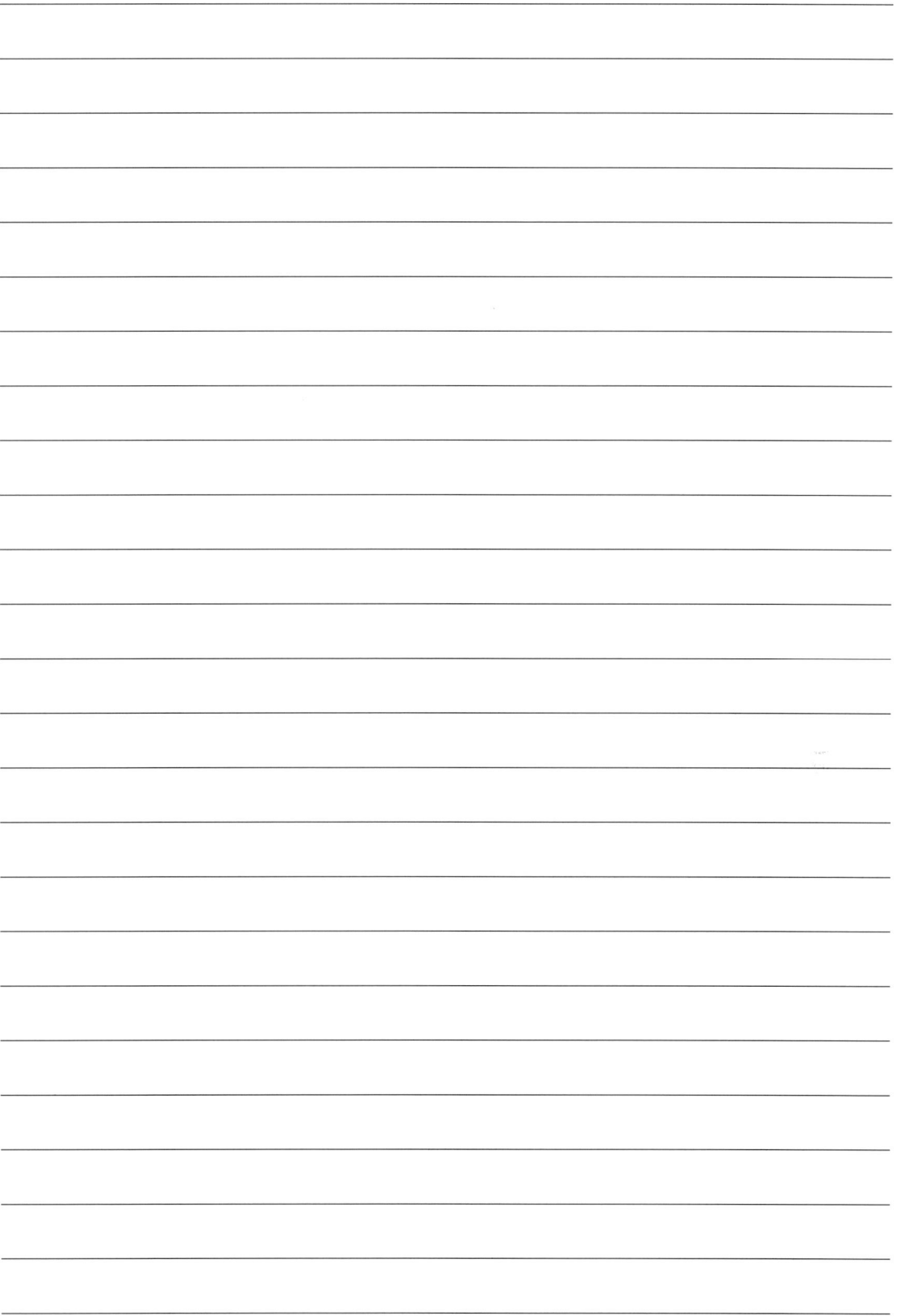

Date:	Anxiety Scale (1-10): AM PM
Today was I compassionate with myself or critical?	Are my thoughts giving me power or taking it away?

Are my thoughts true? *Really true?*

Am I avoiding something that I need to deal with?

Am I forecasting the future?

Am I "catastrophizing"?

Did I experience fear today?	Did it actually come true?
What helps to ease my anxiety?	Did I remember that?
Did I nourish my body and drink enough water?	Did I get fresh air?
How did I move my body today?	Did I try to practice mindfulness and deep breathing?
Did I have "What if's" today?	I am grateful for:

Promise me you'll always remember:
You're braver than you believe, stronger than you seem and smarter than you think.
A.A. Milne

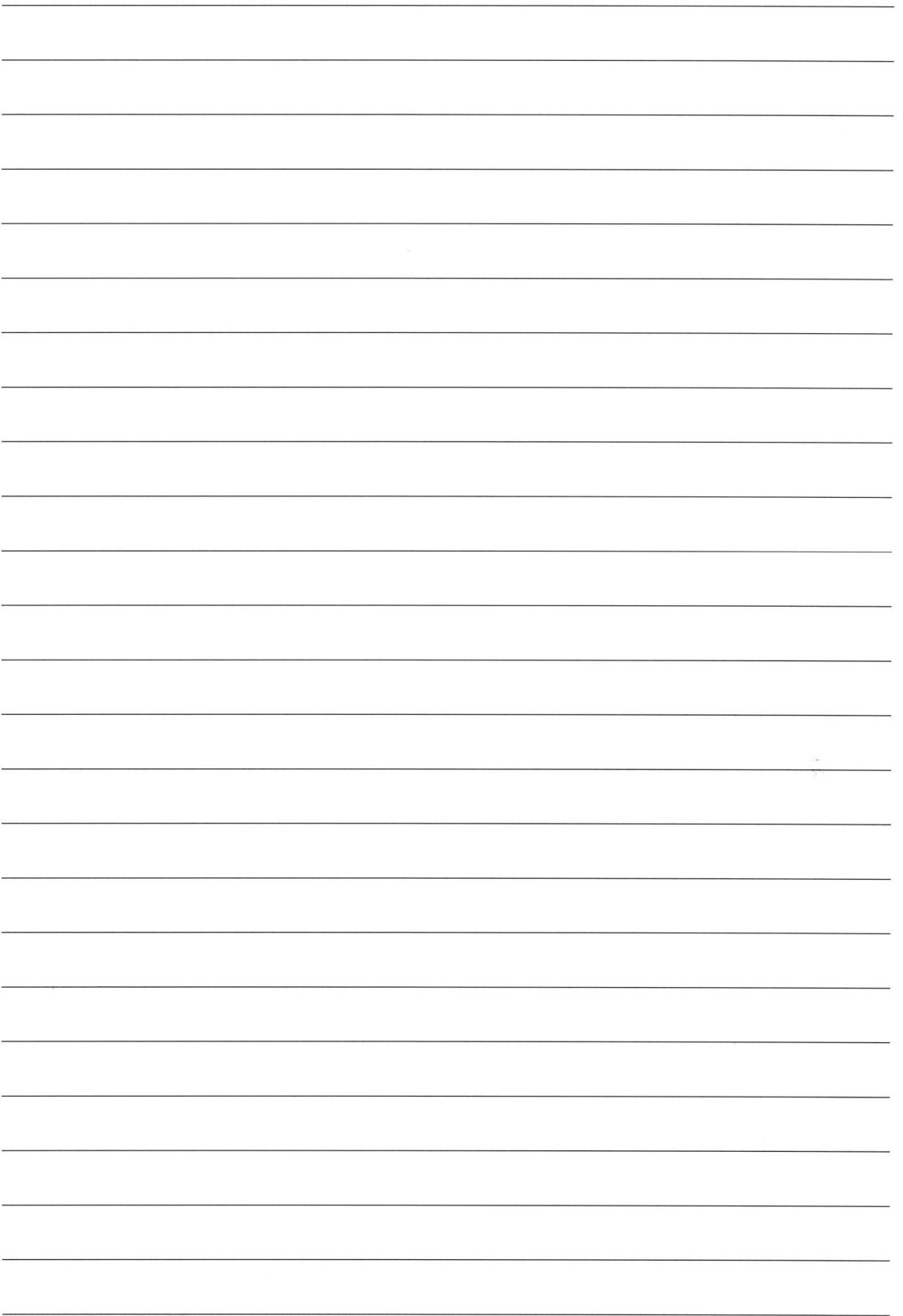

REVIEW OF LAST WEEK

Overall my week was...

Did I have the support I needed?

Did I ask for help when I needed it?

Did I remember my intentions from last week?

Did I spend enough time being unplugged?

I am proud that I....

Notes:

WEEKLY CHECK-IN

My Intention for Next Week:

I would like to:

Experience...

Let go of...

Feel...

Learn to...

Stop...

I want more...	I want less...

Date:	Anxiety Scale (1-10): AM PM
Today was I compassionate with myself or critical?	Are my thoughts giving me power or taking it away?

Are my thoughts true? *Really true?*

Am I avoiding something that I need to deal with?

Am I forecasting the future?

Am I "catastrophizing"?

Did I experience fear today?	Did it actually come true?
What helps to ease my anxiety?	Did I remember that?
Did I nourish my body and drink enough water?	Did I get fresh air?
How did I move my body today?	Did I try to practice mindfulness and deep breathing?
Did I have "What if's" today?	I am grateful for:

Promise me you'll always remember:
You're braver than you believe, stronger than you seem and smarter than you think.
A.A. Milne

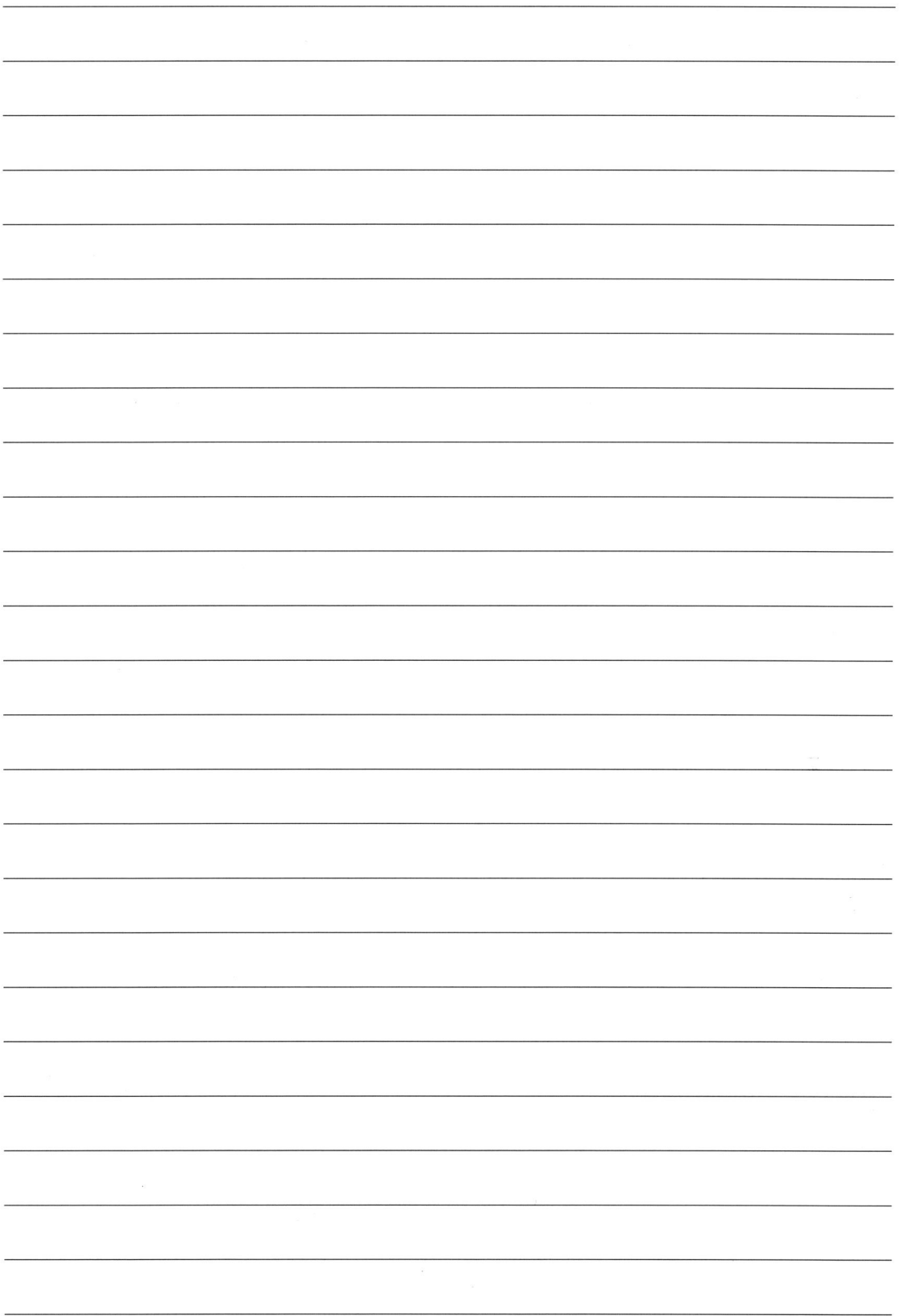

Date:	Anxiety Scale (1-10): AM PM
Today was I compassionate with myself or critical?	Are my thoughts giving me power or taking it away?

Are my thoughts true? *Really true?*

Am I avoiding something that I need to deal with?

Am I forecasting the future?

Am I "catastrophizing"?

Did I experience fear today?	Did it actually come true?
What helps to ease my anxiety?	Did I remember that?
Did I nourish my body and drink enough water?	Did I get fresh air?
How did I move my body today?	Did I try to practice mindfulness and deep breathing?
Did I have "What if's" today?	I am grateful for:

Promise me you'll always remember:
You're braver than you believe, stronger than you seem and smarter than you think.
A.A. Milne

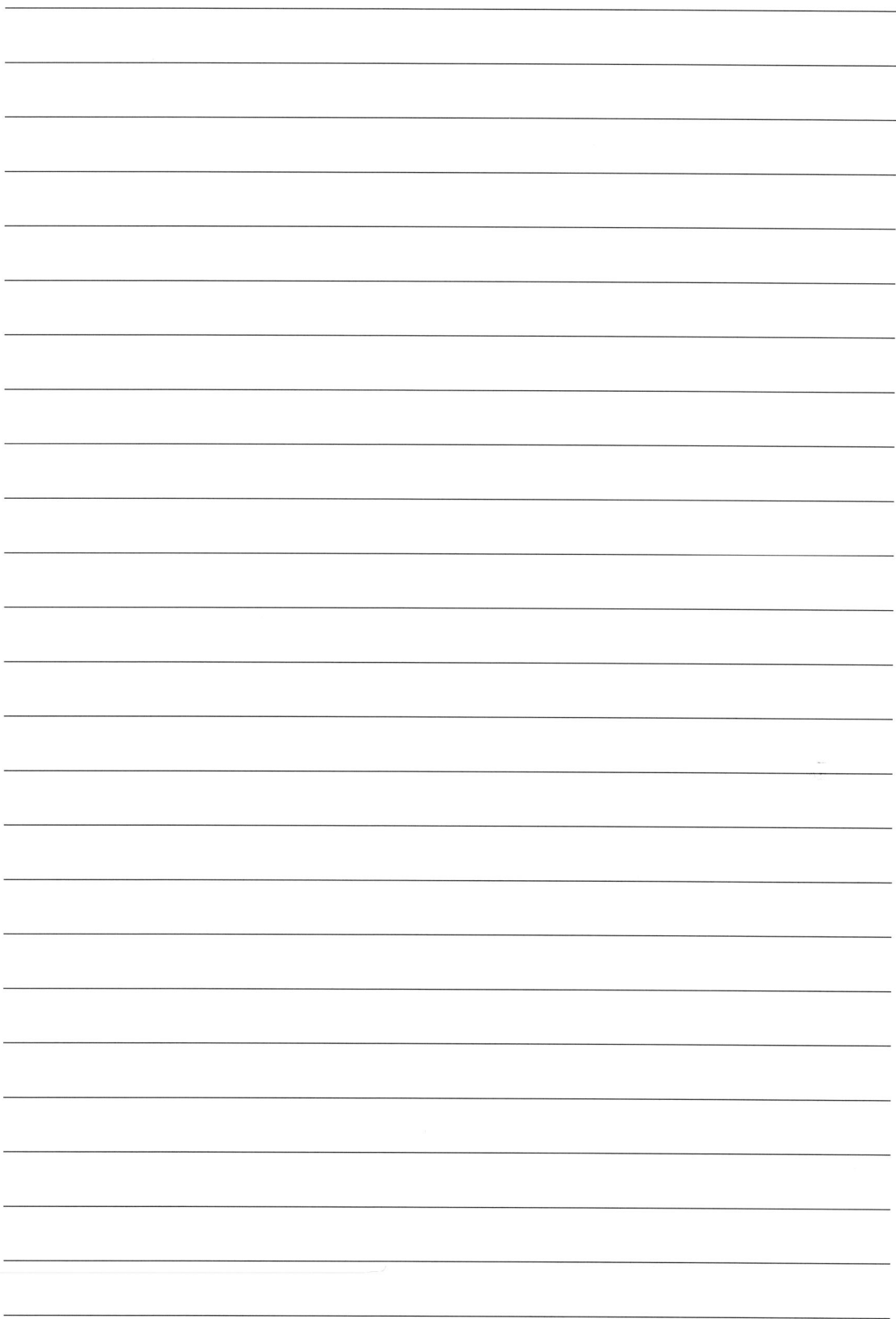

Date:	Anxiety Scale (1-10): AM PM
Today was I compassionate with myself or critical?	Are my thoughts giving me power or taking it away?

Are my thoughts true? *Really true?*

Am I avoiding something that I need to deal with?

Am I forecasting the future?

Am I "catastrophizing"?

Did I experience fear today?	Did it actually come true?
What helps to ease my anxiety?	Did I remember that?
Did I nourish my body and drink enough water?	Did I get fresh air?
How did I move my body today?	Did I try to practice mindfulness and deep breathing?
Did I have "What if's" today?	I am grateful for:

Promise me you'll always remember:
You're braver than you believe, stronger than you seem and smarter than you think.
A.A. Milne

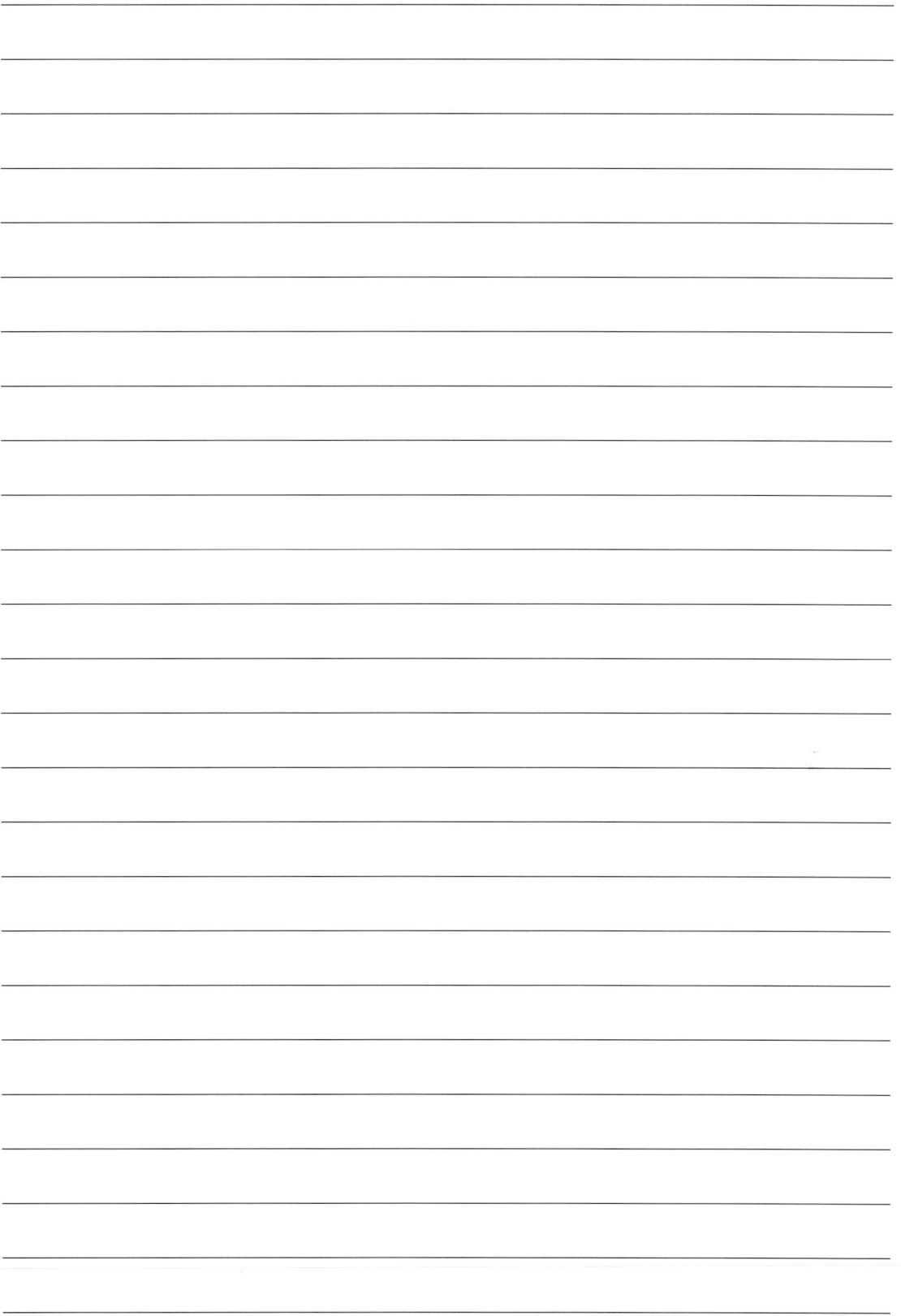

| Date: | Anxiety Scale (1-10): |
| | AM   PM |

| Today was I compassionate with myself or critical? | Are my thoughts giving me power or taking it away? |

Are my thoughts true? *Really true?*

Am I avoiding something that I need to deal with?

Am I forecasting the future?

Am I "catastrophizing"?

| Did I experience fear today? | Did it actually come true? |

| What helps to ease my anxiety? | Did I remember that? |

| Did I nourish my body and drink enough water? | Did I get fresh air? |

| How did I move my body today? | Did I try to practice mindfulness and deep breathing? |

| Did I have "What if's" today? | I am grateful for: |

Promise me you'll always remember:
You're braver than you believe, stronger than you seem and smarter than you think.
A.A. Milne

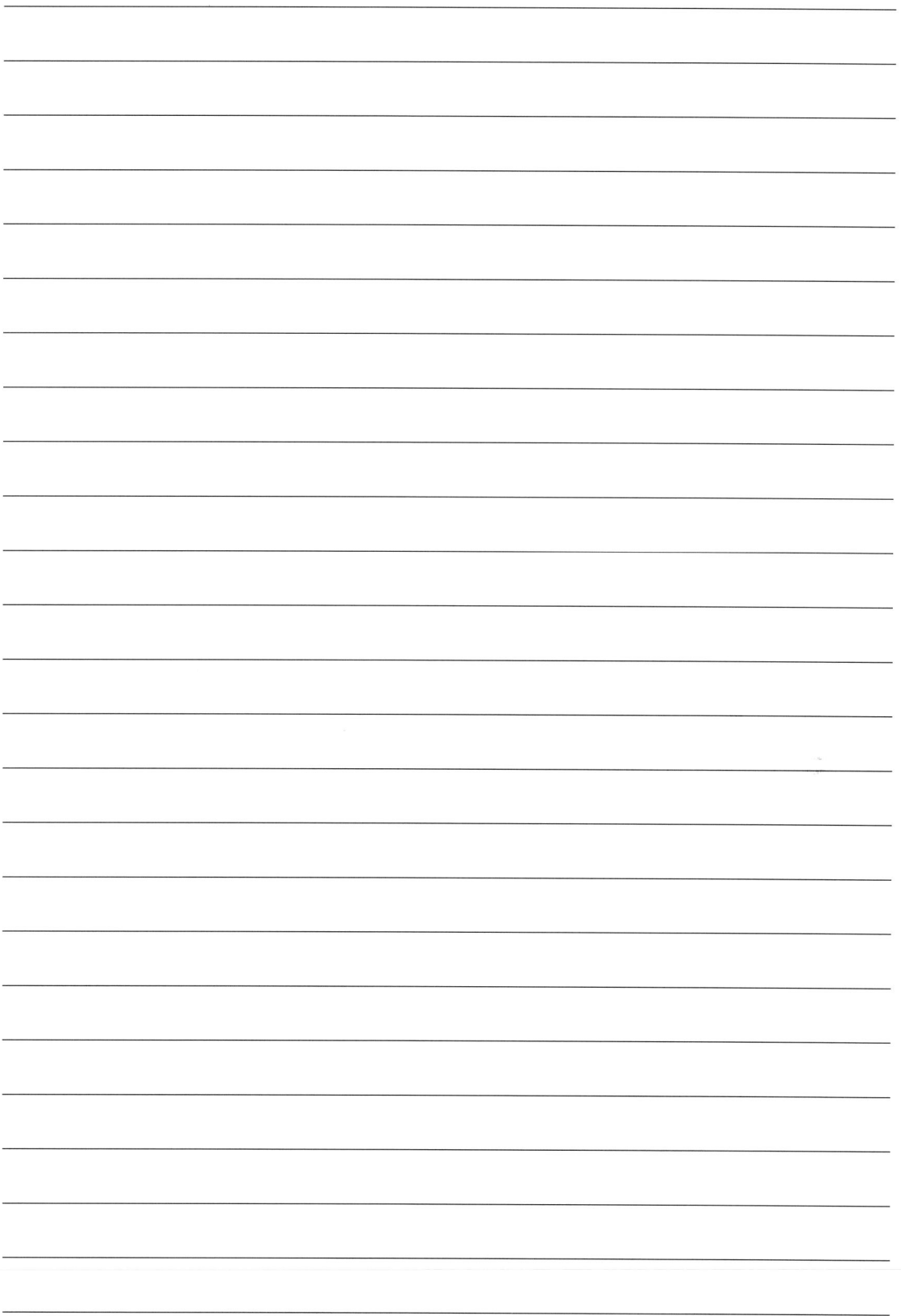

Date:	Anxiety Scale (1-10): AM PM
Today was I compassionate with myself or critical?	Are my thoughts giving me power or taking it away?

Are my thoughts true? *Really true?*

Am I avoiding something that I need to deal with?

Am I forecasting the future?

Am I "catastrophizing"?

Did I experience fear today?	Did it actually come true?
What helps to ease my anxiety?	Did I remember that?
Did I nourish my body and drink enough water?	Did I get fresh air?
How did I move my body today?	Did I try to practice mindfulness and deep breathing?
Did I have "What if's" today?	I am grateful for:

Promise me you'll always remember:
You're braver than you believe, stronger than you seem and smarter than you think.
A.A. Milne

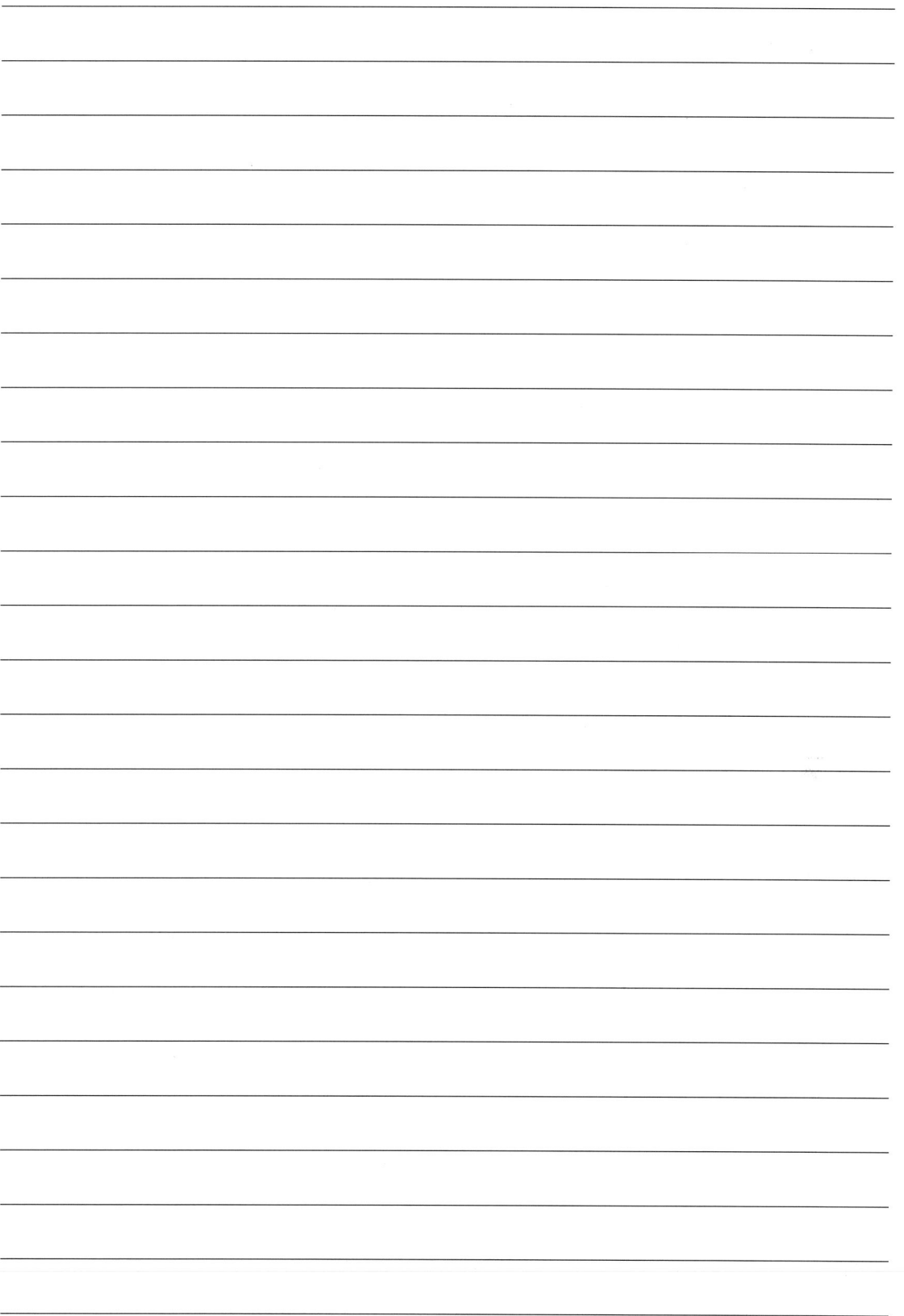

Date:	Anxiety Scale (1-10): AM PM
Today was I compassionate with myself or critical?	Are my thoughts giving me power or taking it away?

Are my thoughts true? *Really true?*

Am I avoiding something that I need to deal with?

Am I forecasting the future?

Am I "catastrophizing"?

Did I experience fear today?	Did it actually come true?
What helps to ease my anxiety?	Did I remember that?
Did I nourish my body and drink enough water?	Did I get fresh air?
How did I move my body today?	Did I try to practice mindfulness and deep breathing?
Did I have "What if's" today?	I am grateful for:

Promise me you'll always remember:
You're braver than you believe, stronger than you seem and smarter than you think.
A.A. Milne

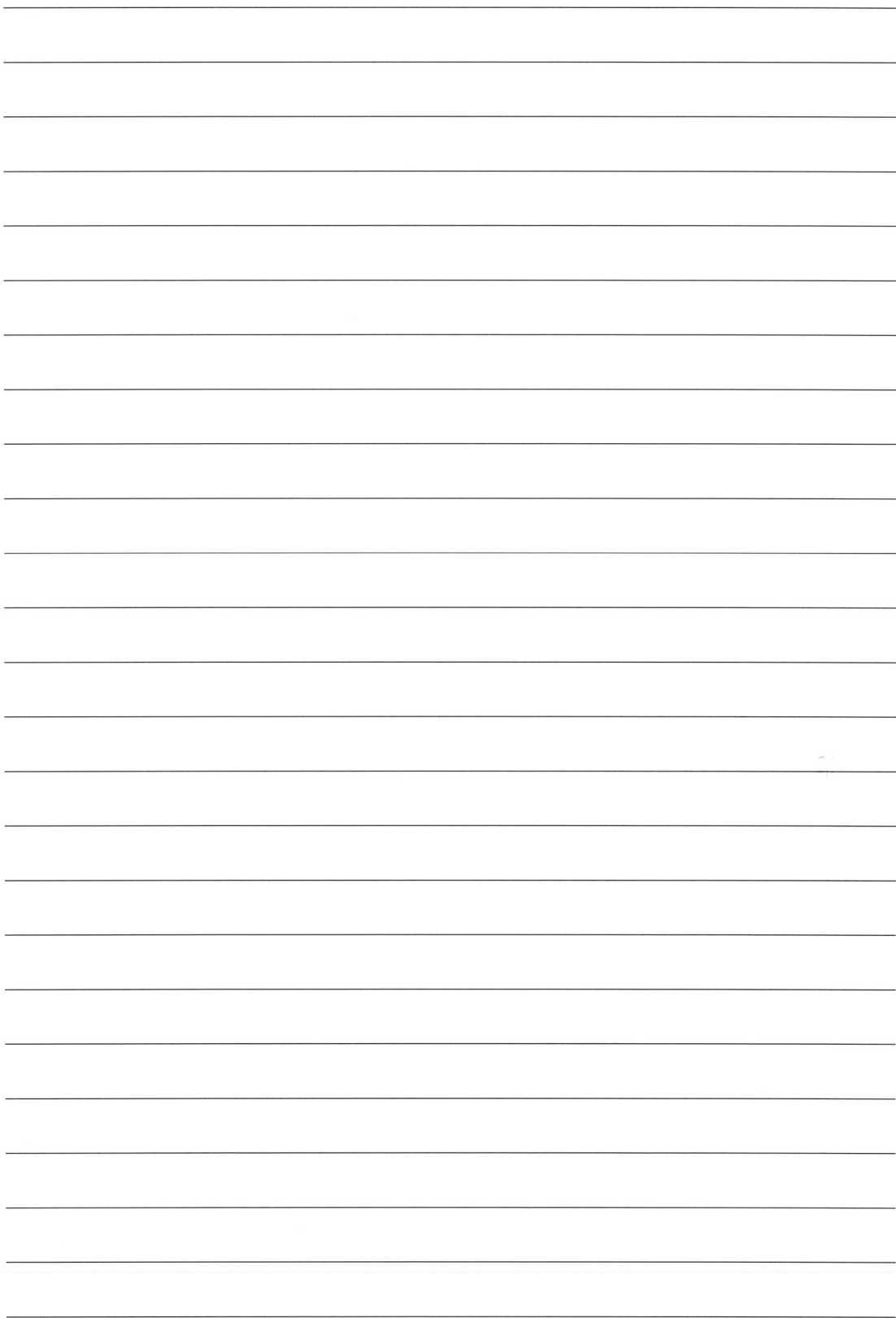

Date:	Anxiety Scale (1-10): AM PM
Today was I compassionate with myself or critical?	Are my thoughts giving me power or taking it away?

Are my thoughts true? *Really true?*

Am I avoiding something that I need to deal with?

Am I forecasting the future?

Am I "catastrophizing"?

Did I experience fear today?	Did it actually come true?
What helps to ease my anxiety?	Did I remember that?
Did I nourish my body and drink enough water?	Did I get fresh air?
How did I move my body today?	Did I try to practice mindfulness and deep breathing?
Did I have "What if's" today?	I am grateful for:

Promise me you'll always remember:
You're braver than you believe, stronger than you seem and smarter than you think.
A.A. Milne

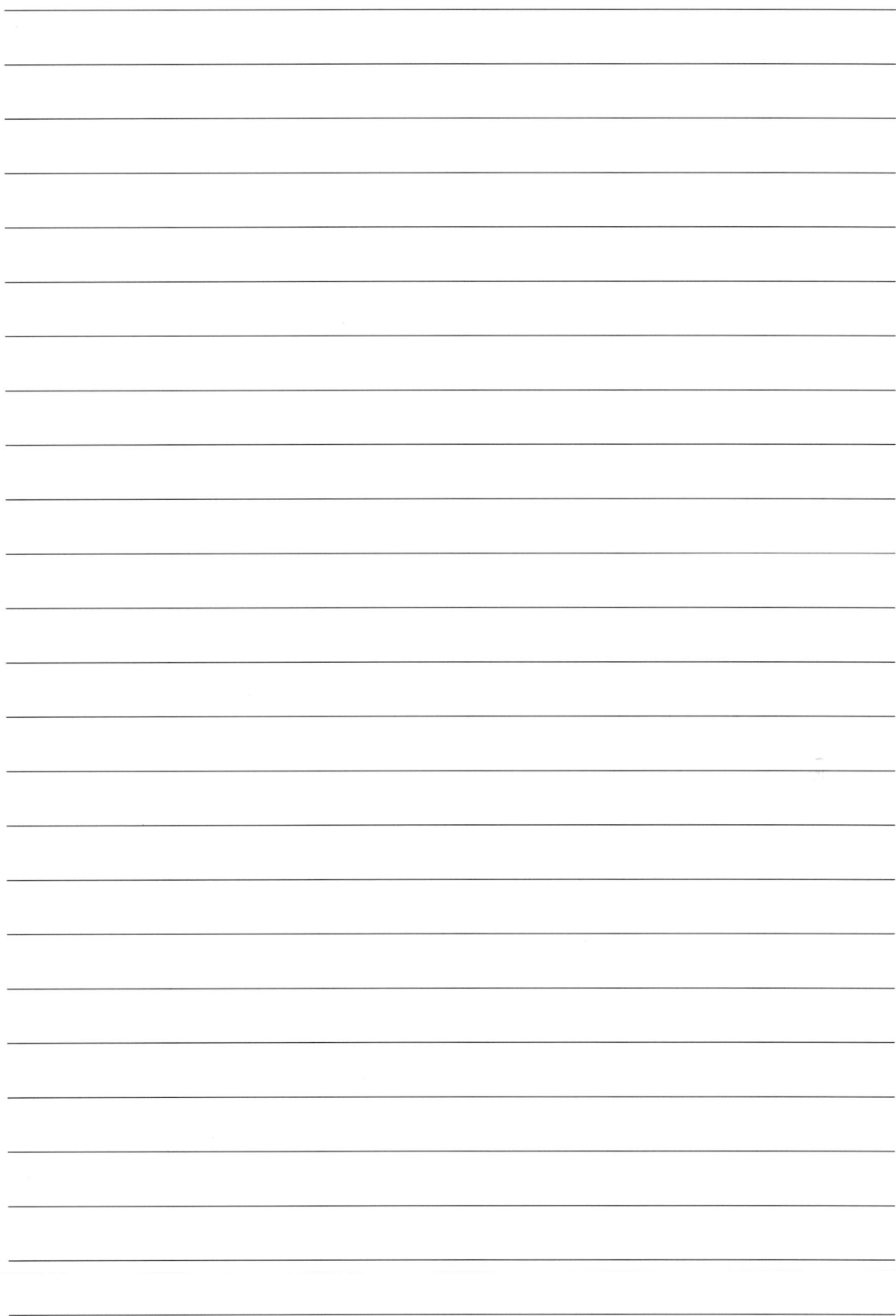

REVIEW OF LAST WEEK

Overall my week was...

Did I have the support I needed?

Did I ask for help when I needed it?

Did I remember my intentions from last week?

Did I spend enough time being unplugged?

I am proud that I....

Notes:

WEEKLY CHECK-IN

My Intention for Next Week:

I would like to:

Experience...

Let go of...

Feel...

Learn to...

Stop...

I want more...	I want less...

Date:	Anxiety Scale (1-10): AM PM
Today was I compassionate with myself or critical?	Are my thoughts giving me power or taking it away?

Are my thoughts true? *Really true?*

Am I avoiding something that I need to deal with?

Am I forecasting the future?

Am I "catastrophizing"?

Did I experience fear today?	Did it actually come true?
What helps to ease my anxiety?	Did I remember that?
Did I nourish my body and drink enough water?	Did I get fresh air?
How did I move my body today?	Did I try to practice mindfulness and deep breathing?
Did I have "What if's" today?	I am grateful for:

Promise me you'll always remember:
You're braver than you believe, stronger than you seem and smarter than you think.
A.A. Milne

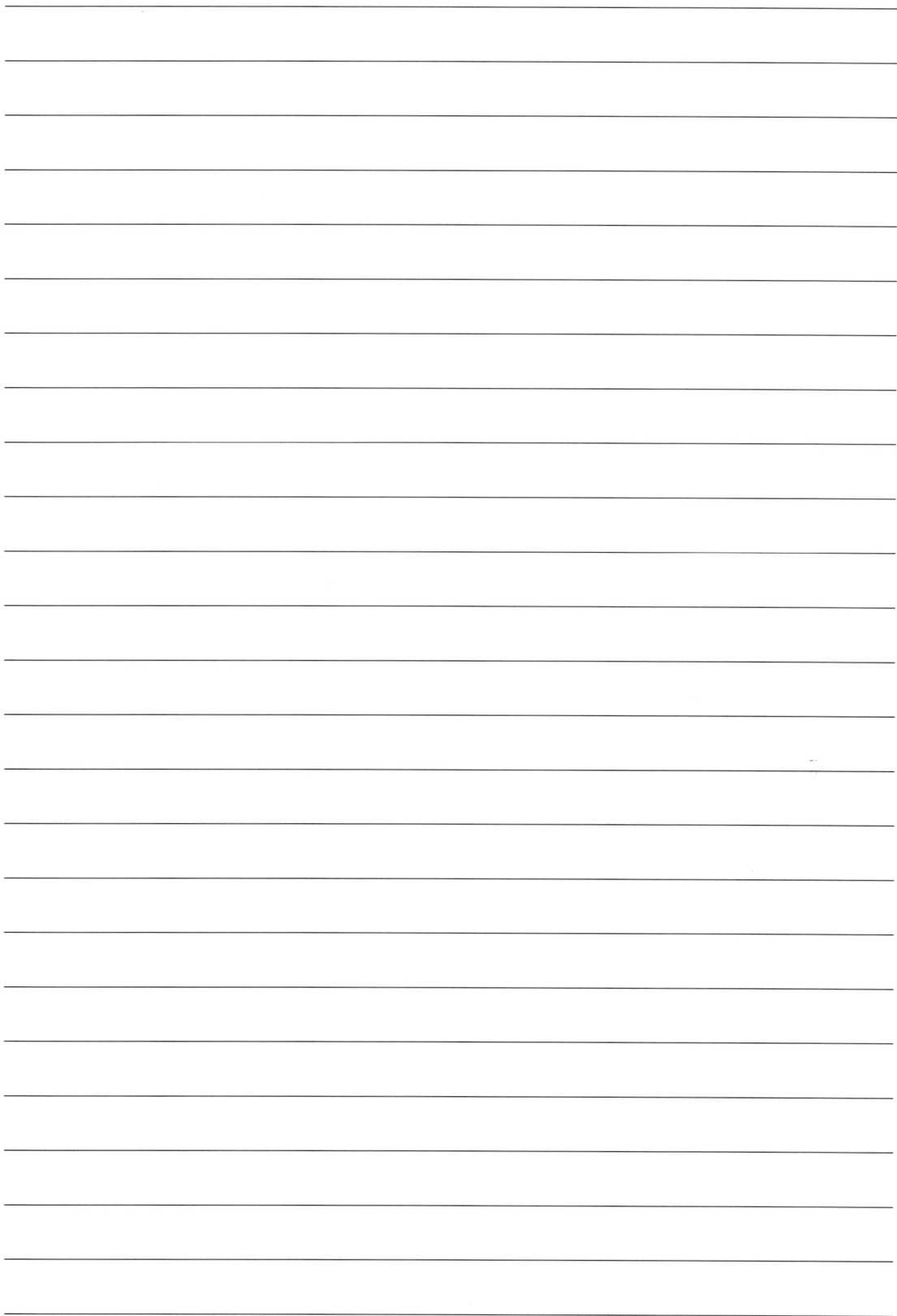

Date:	Anxiety Scale (1-10): AM PM
Today was I compassionate with myself or critical?	Are my thoughts giving me power or taking it away?

Are my thoughts true? *Really true?*

Am I avoiding something that I need to deal with?

Am I forecasting the future?

Am I "catastrophizing"?

Did I experience fear today?	Did it actually come true?
What helps to ease my anxiety?	Did I remember that?
Did I nourish my body and drink enough water?	Did I get fresh air?
How did I move my body today?	Did I try to practice mindfulness and deep breathing?
Did I have "What if's" today?	I am grateful for:

Promise me you'll always remember:
You're braver than you believe, stronger than you seem and smarter than you think.
A.A. Milne

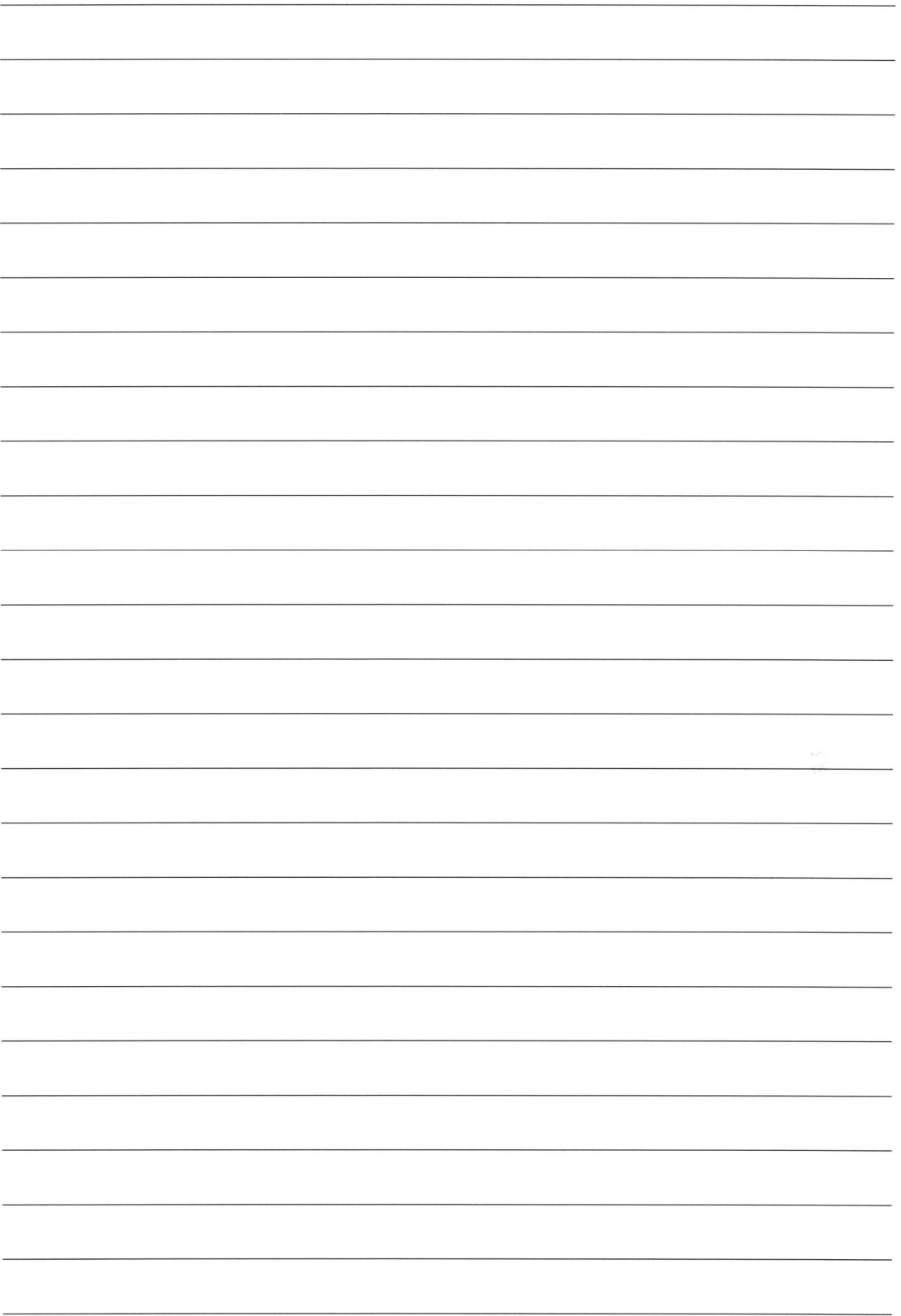

Date:	Anxiety Scale (1-10): AM PM
Today was I compassionate with myself or critical?	Are my thoughts giving me power or taking it away?

Are my thoughts true? *Really true?*

Am I avoiding something that I need to deal with?

Am I forecasting the future?

Am I "catastrophizing"?

Did I experience fear today?	Did it actually come true?
What helps to ease my anxiety?	Did I remember that?
Did I nourish my body and drink enough water?	Did I get fresh air?
How did I move my body today?	Did I try to practice mindfulness and deep breathing?
Did I have "What if's" today?	I am grateful for:

Promise me you'll always remember:
You're braver than you believe, stronger than you seem and smarter than you think.
A.A. Milne

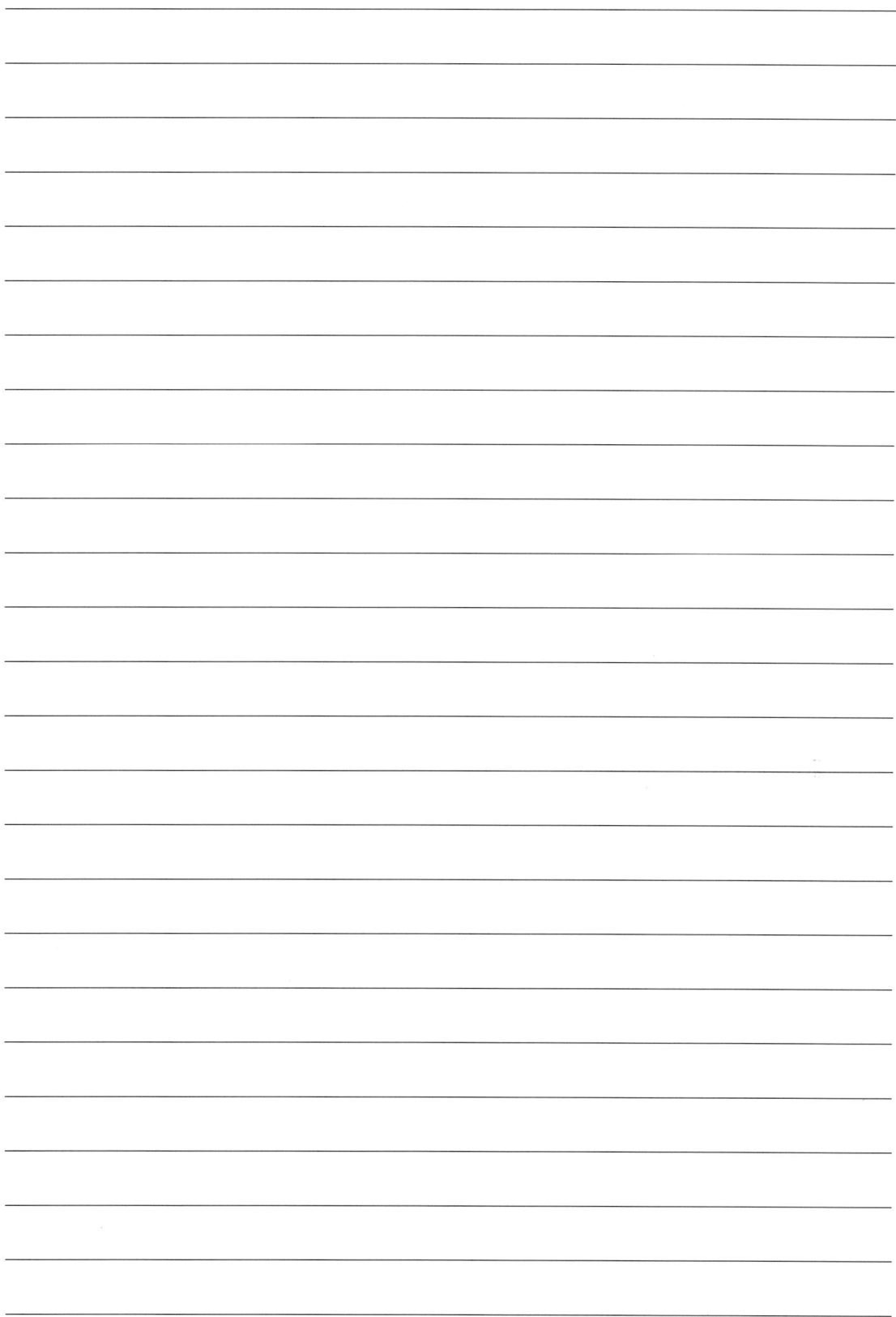

Date:	Anxiety Scale (1-10): AM PM
Today was I compassionate with myself or critical?	Are my thoughts giving me power or taking it away?

Are my thoughts true? *Really true?*

Am I avoiding something that I need to deal with?

Am I forecasting the future?

Am I "catastrophizing"?

Did I experience fear today?	Did it actually come true?
What helps to ease my anxiety?	Did I remember that?
Did I nourish my body and drink enough water?	Did I get fresh air?
How did I move my body today?	Did I try to practice mindfulness and deep breathing?
Did I have "What if's" today?	I am grateful for:

Promise me you'll always remember:
You're braver than you believe, stronger than you seem and smarter than you think.
A.A. Milne

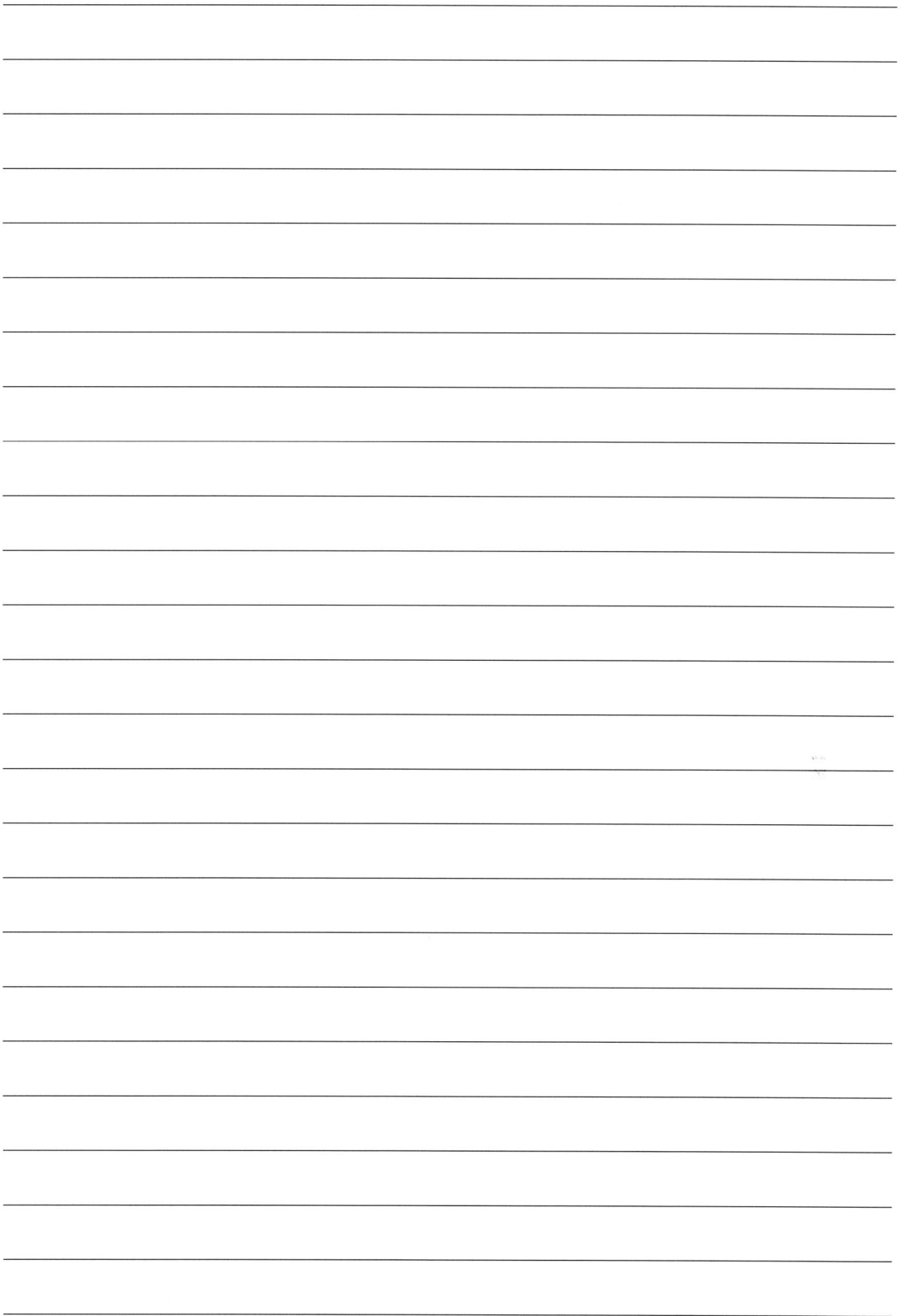

Date:	Anxiety Scale (1-10): AM PM
Today was I compassionate with myself or critical?	Are my thoughts giving me power or taking it away?

Are my thoughts true? *Really true?*

Am I avoiding something that I need to deal with?

Am I forecasting the future?

Am I "catastrophizing"?

Did I experience fear today?	Did it actually come true?
What helps to ease my anxiety?	Did I remember that?
Did I nourish my body and drink enough water?	Did I get fresh air?
How did I move my body today?	Did I try to practice mindfulness and deep breathing?
Did I have "What if's" today?	I am grateful for:

Promise me you'll always remember:
You're braver than you believe, stronger than you seem and smarter than you think.
A.A. Milne

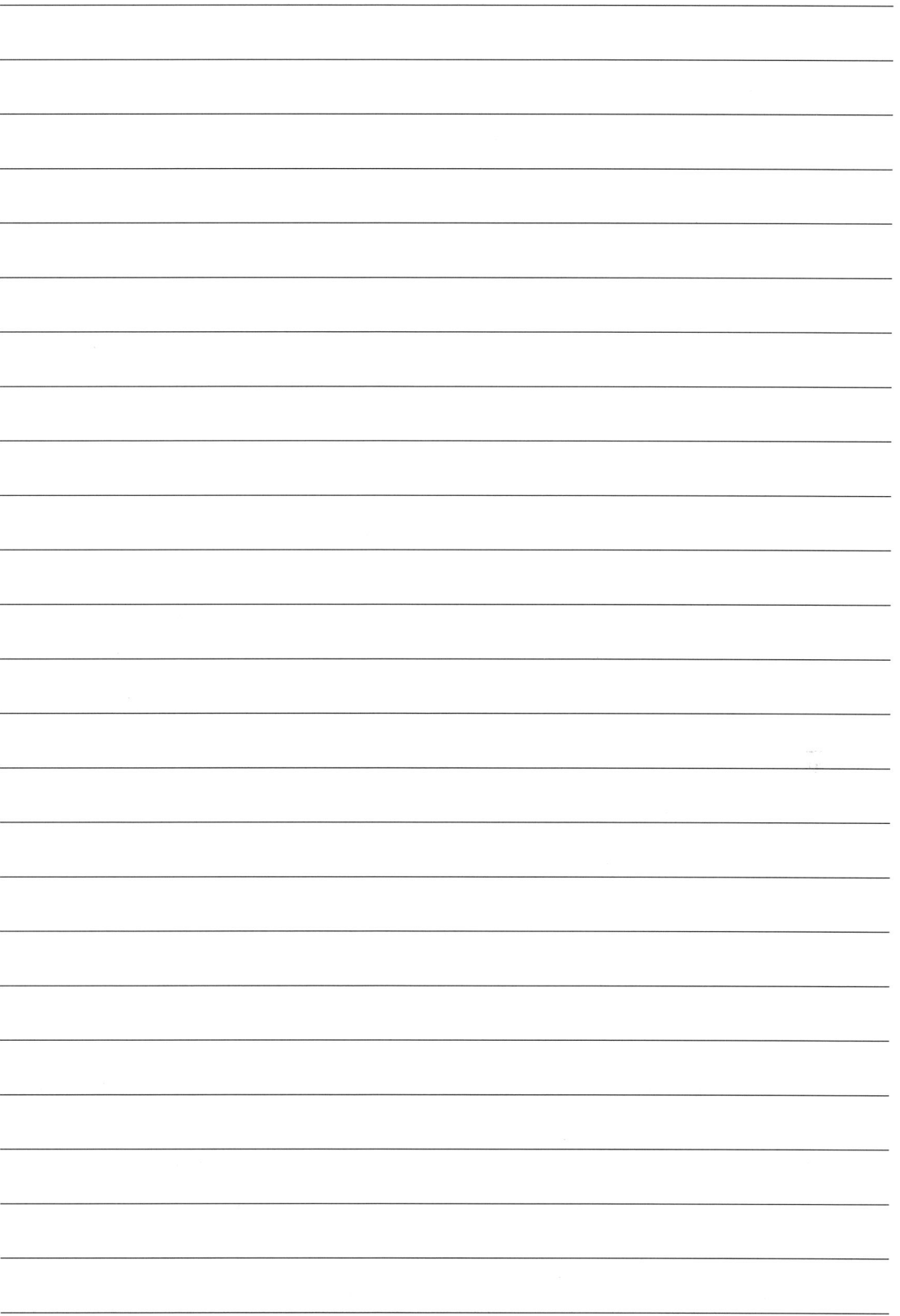

Date:	Anxiety Scale (1-10): AM PM
Today was I compassionate with myself or critical?	Are my thoughts giving me power or taking it away?

Are my thoughts true? *Really true?*

Am I avoiding something that I need to deal with?

Am I forecasting the future?

Am I "catastrophizing"?

Did I experience fear today?	Did it actually come true?
What helps to ease my anxiety?	Did I remember that?
Did I nourish my body and drink enough water?	Did I get fresh air?
How did I move my body today?	Did I try to practice mindfulness and deep breathing?
Did I have "What if's" today?	I am grateful for:

Promise me you'll always remember:
You're braver than you believe, stronger than you seem and smarter than you think.
A.A. Milne

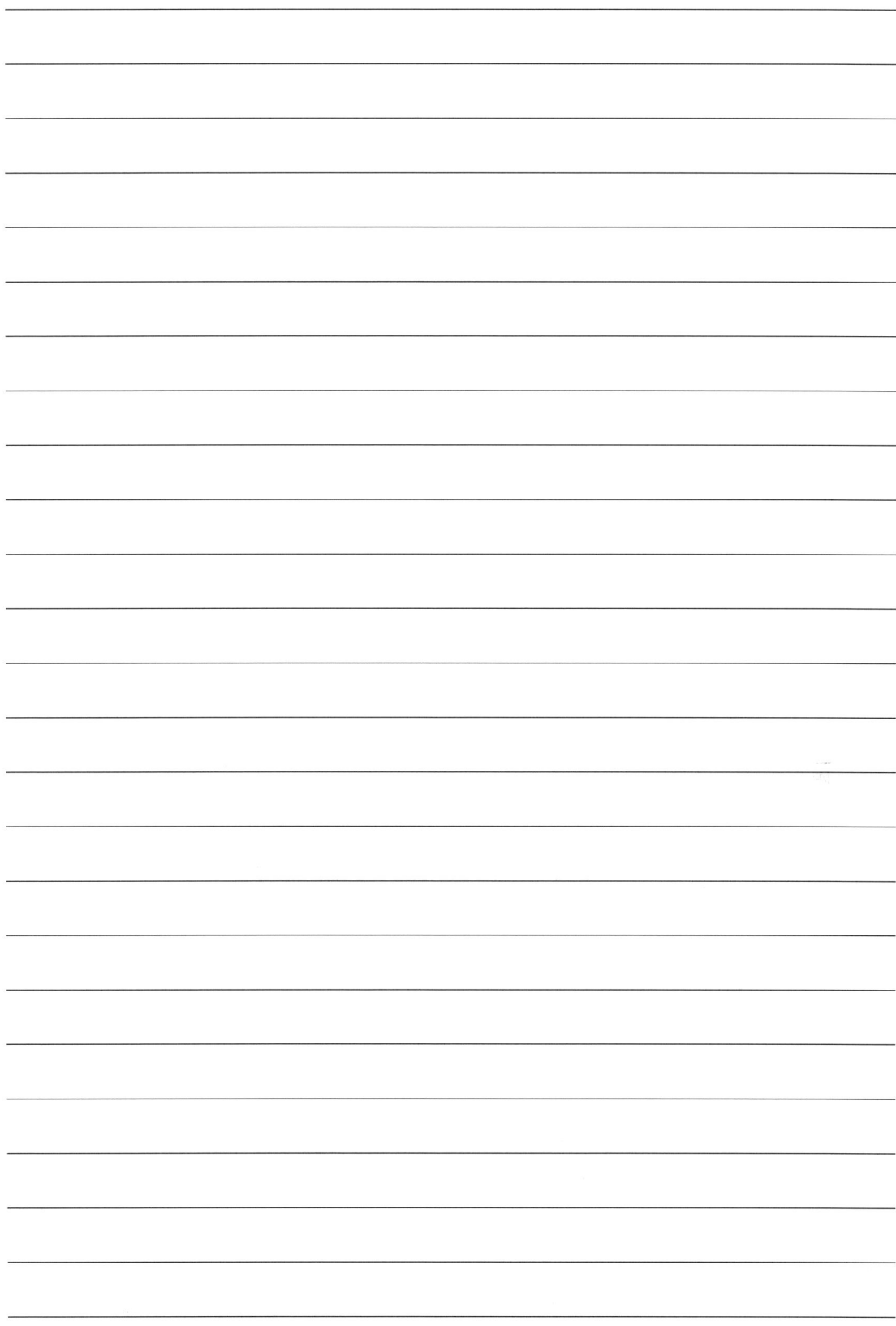

Date:	Anxiety Scale (1-10): AM PM
Today was I compassionate with myself or critical?	Are my thoughts giving me power or taking it away?

Are my thoughts true? *Really true?*

Am I avoiding something that I need to deal with?

Am I forecasting the future?

Am I "catastrophizing"?

Did I experience fear today?	Did it actually come true?
What helps to ease my anxiety?	Did I remember that?
Did I nourish my body and drink enough water?	Did I get fresh air?
How did I move my body today?	Did I try to practice mindfulness and deep breathing?
Did I have "What if's" today?	I am grateful for:

Promise me you'll always remember:
You're braver than you believe, stronger than you seem and smarter than you think.
A.A. Milne

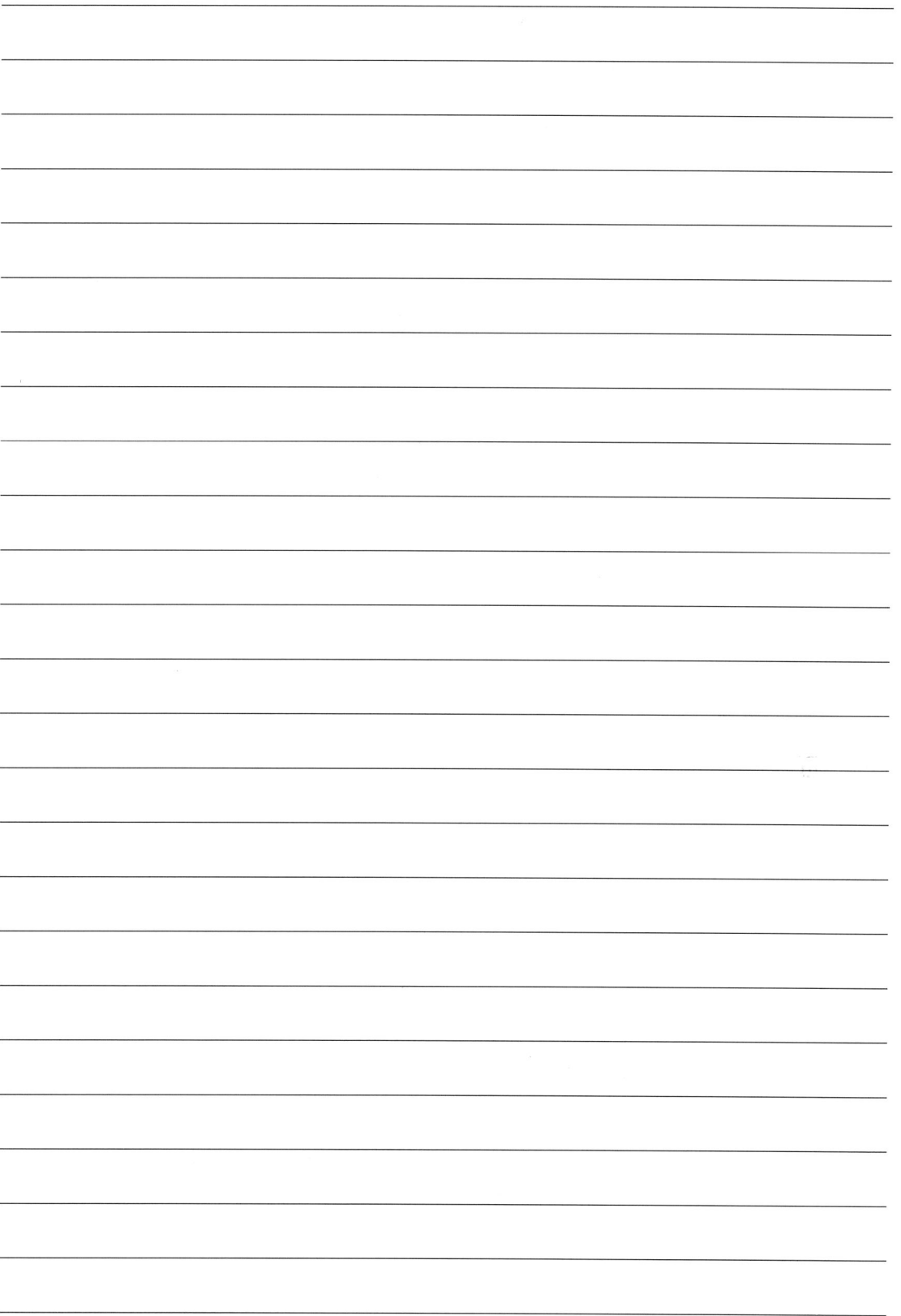

REVIEW OF LAST WEEK

Overall my week was...

Did I have the support I needed? | Did I ask for help when I needed it?

Did I remember my intentions from last week?

Did I spend enough time being unplugged?

I am proud that I....

Notes:

WEEKLY CHECK-IN

My Intention for Next Week:

I would like to:

Experience...

Let go of...

Feel...

Learn to...

Stop...

I want more...	I want less...

Date:	Anxiety Scale (1-10): AM PM
Today was I compassionate with myself or critical?	Are my thoughts giving me power or taking it away?

Are my thoughts true? *Really true?*

Am I avoiding something that I need to deal with?

Am I forecasting the future?

Am I "catastrophizing"?

Did I experience fear today?	Did it actually come true?
What helps to ease my anxiety?	Did I remember that?
Did I nourish my body and drink enough water?	Did I get fresh air?
How did I move my body today?	Did I try to practice mindfulness and deep breathing?
Did I have "What if's" today?	I am grateful for:

Promise me you'll always remember:
You're braver than you believe, stronger than you seem and smarter than you think.
A.A. Milne

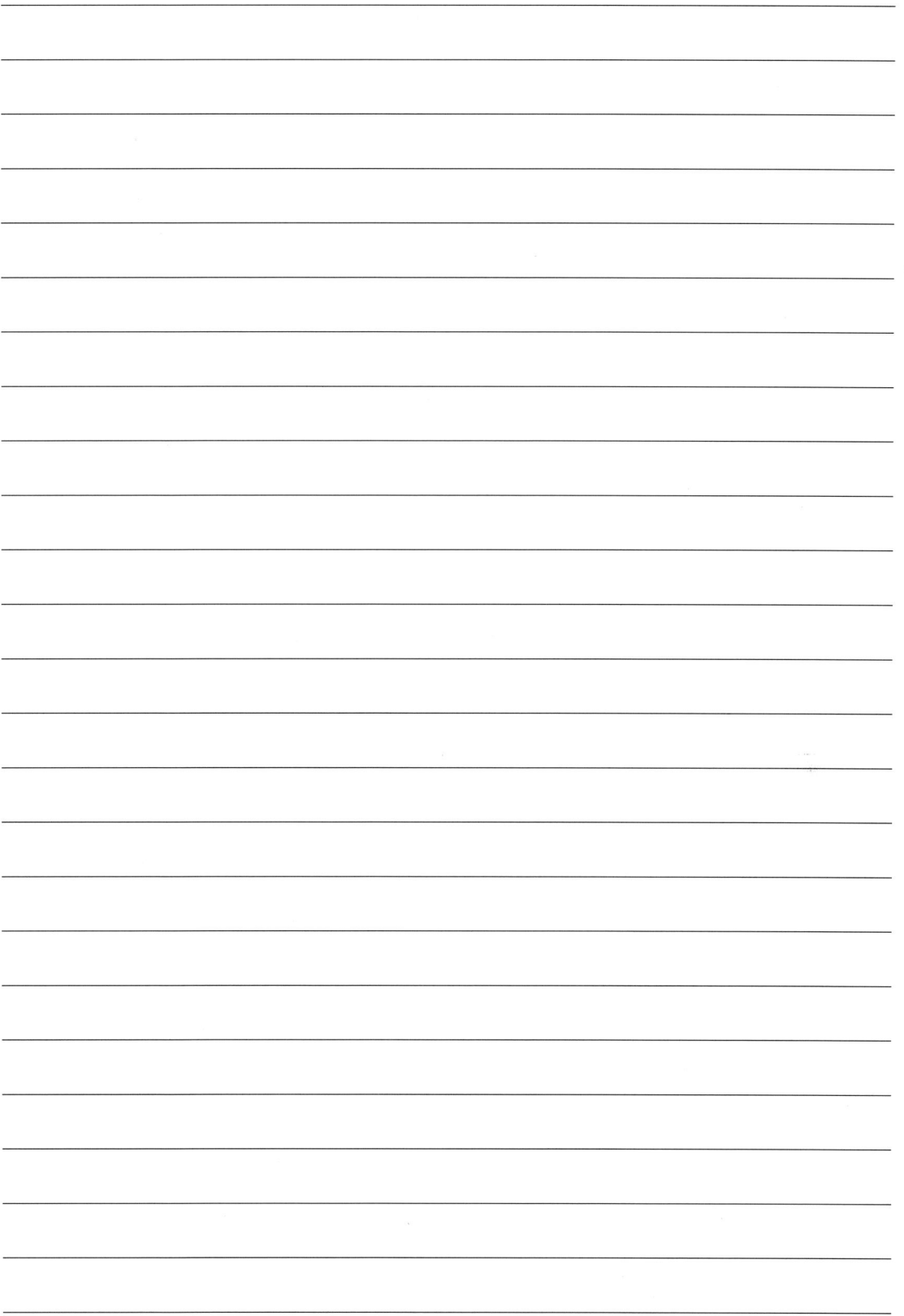

Date:	Anxiety Scale (1-10): AM PM
Today was I compassionate with myself or critical?	Are my thoughts giving me power or taking it away?

Are my thoughts true? *Really true?*

Am I avoiding something that I need to deal with?

Am I forecasting the future?

Am I "catastrophizing"?

Did I experience fear today?	Did it actually come true?
What helps to ease my anxiety?	Did I remember that?
Did I nourish my body and drink enough water?	Did I get fresh air?
How did I move my body today?	Did I try to practice mindfulness and deep breathing?
Did I have "What if's" today?	I am grateful for:

Promise me you'll always remember:
You're braver than you believe, stronger than you seem and smarter than you think.
A.A. Milne

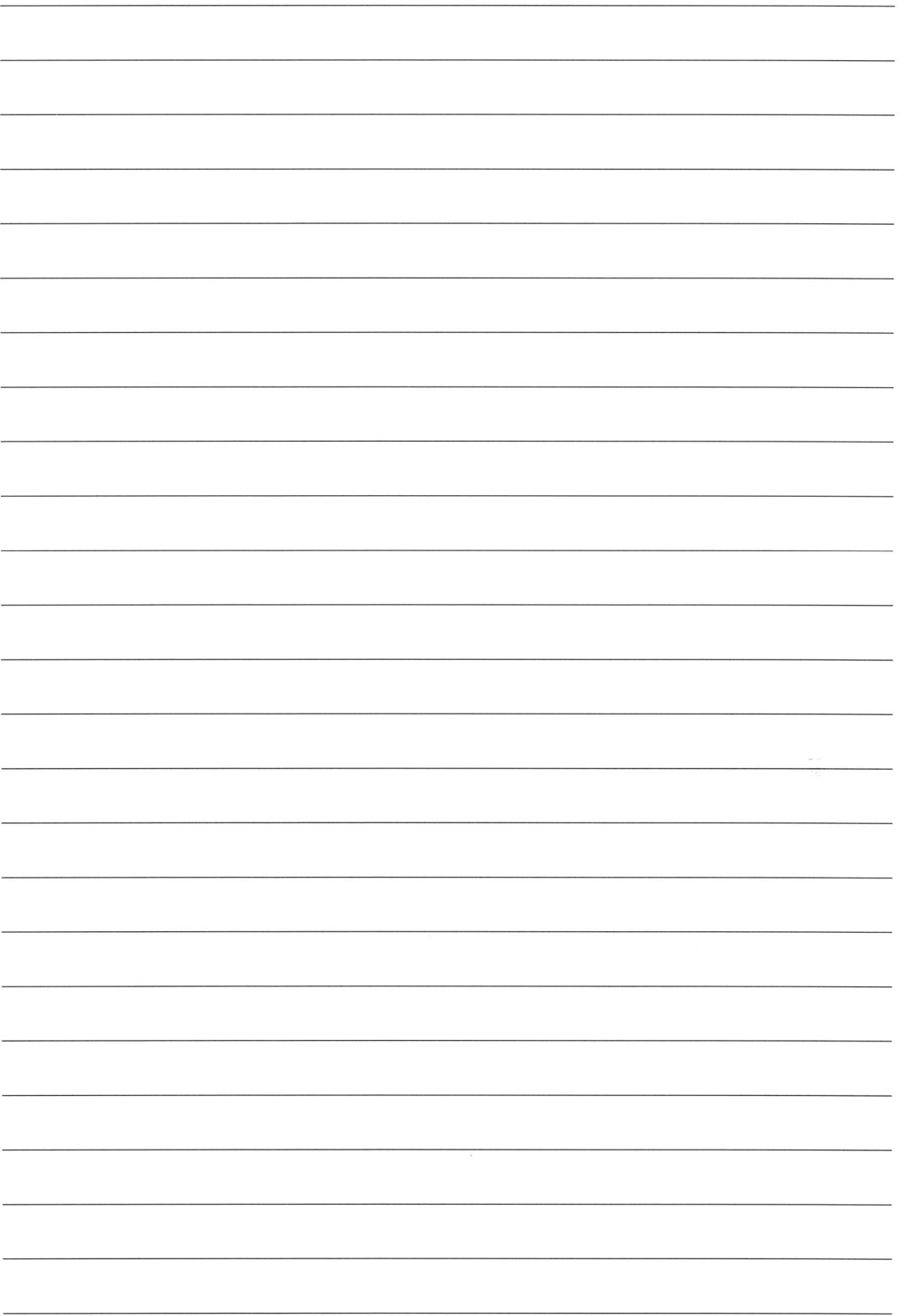

| Date: | Anxiety Scale (1-10): |
	AM PM
Today was I compassionate with myself or critical?	Are my thoughts giving me power or taking it away?

Are my thoughts true? *Really true?*

Am I avoiding something that I need to deal with?

Am I forecasting the future?

Am I "catastrophizing"?

Did I experience fear today?	Did it actually come true?
What helps to ease my anxiety?	Did I remember that?
Did I nourish my body and drink enough water?	Did I get fresh air?
How did I move my body today?	Did I try to practice mindfulness and deep breathing?
Did I have "What if's" today?	I am grateful for:

Promise me you'll always remember:
You're braver than you believe, stronger than you seem and smarter than you think.
A.A. Milne

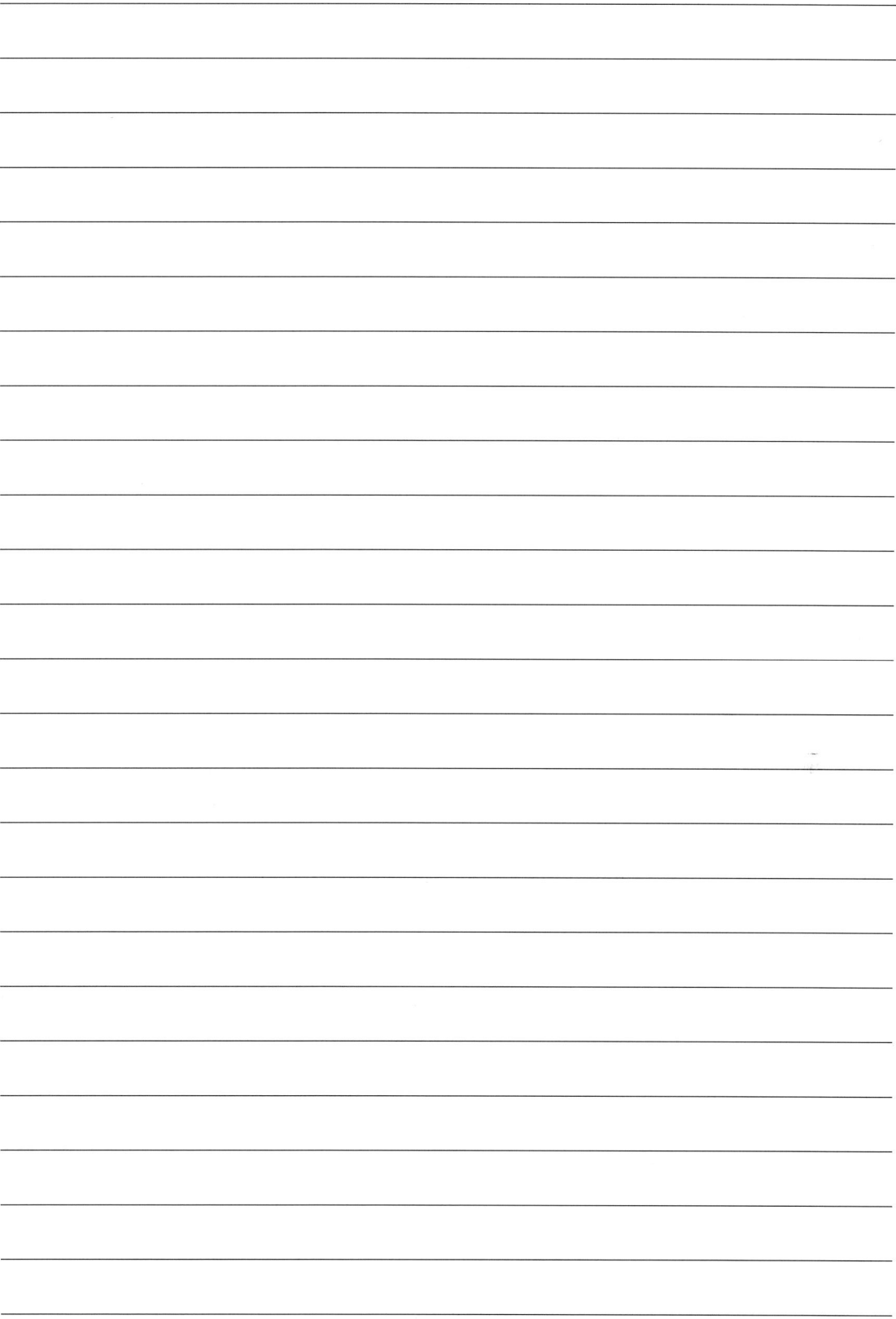

Date:	Anxiety Scale (1-10): AM PM
Today was I compassionate with myself or critical?	Are my thoughts giving me power or taking it away?

Are my thoughts true? *Really true?*

Am I avoiding something that I need to deal with?

Am I forecasting the future?

Am I "catastrophizing"?

Did I experience fear today?	Did it actually come true?
What helps to ease my anxiety?	Did I remember that?
Did I nourish my body and drink enough water?	Did I get fresh air?
How did I move my body today?	Did I try to practice mindfulness and deep breathing?
Did I have "What if's" today?	I am grateful for:

Promise me you'll always remember:
You're braver than you believe, stronger than you seem and smarter than you think.
A.A. Milne

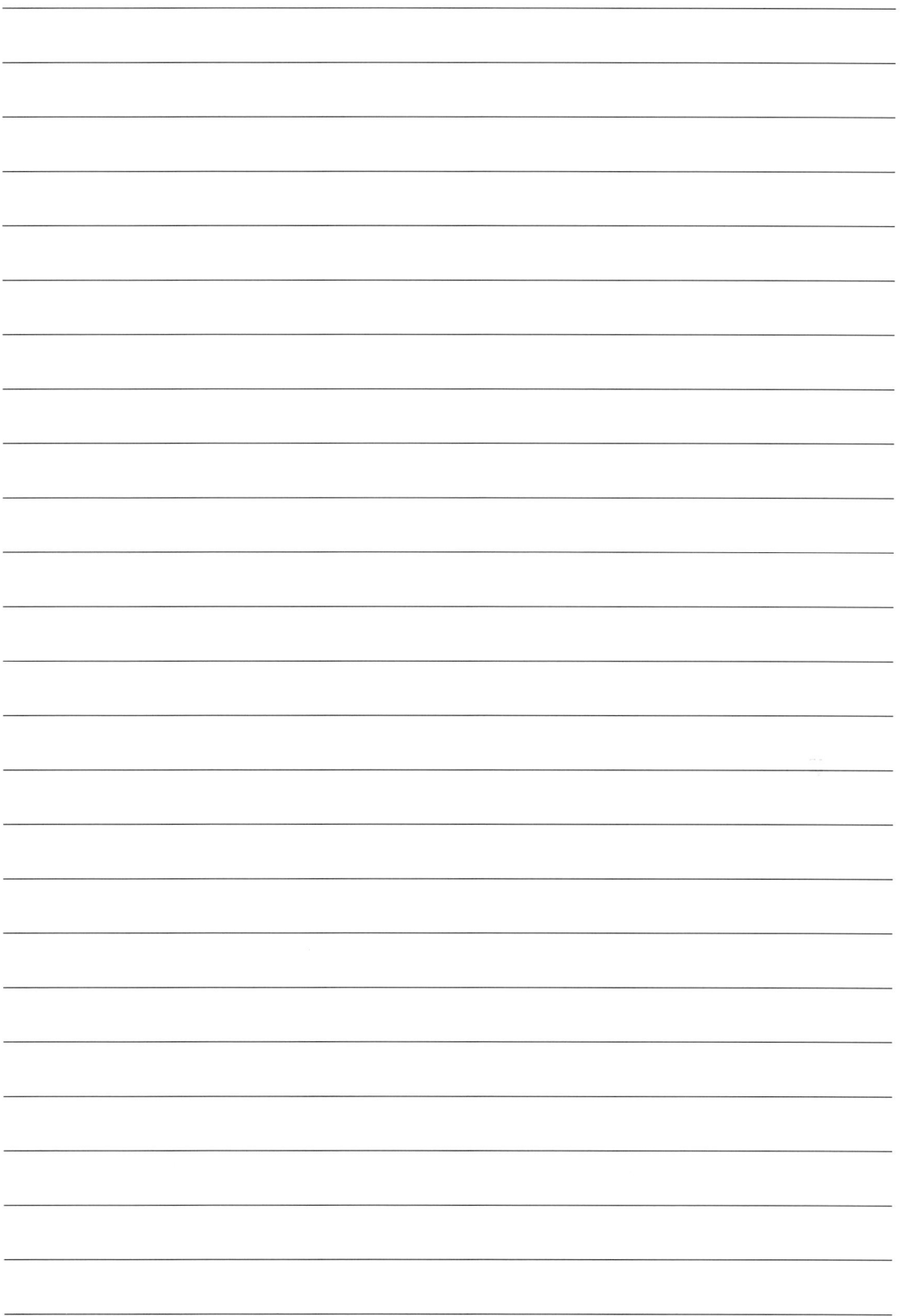

Date:	Anxiety Scale (1-10): AM PM
Today was I compassionate with myself or critical?	Are my thoughts giving me power or taking it away?

Are my thoughts true? *Really true?*

Am I avoiding something that I need to deal with?

Am I forecasting the future?

Am I "catastrophizing"?

Did I experience fear today?	Did it actually come true?
What helps to ease my anxiety?	Did I remember that?
Did I nourish my body and drink enough water?	Did I get fresh air?
How did I move my body today?	Did I try to practice mindfulness and deep breathing?
Did I have "What if's" today?	I am grateful for:

Promise me you'll always remember:
You're braver than you believe, stronger than you seem and smarter than you think.
A.A. Milne

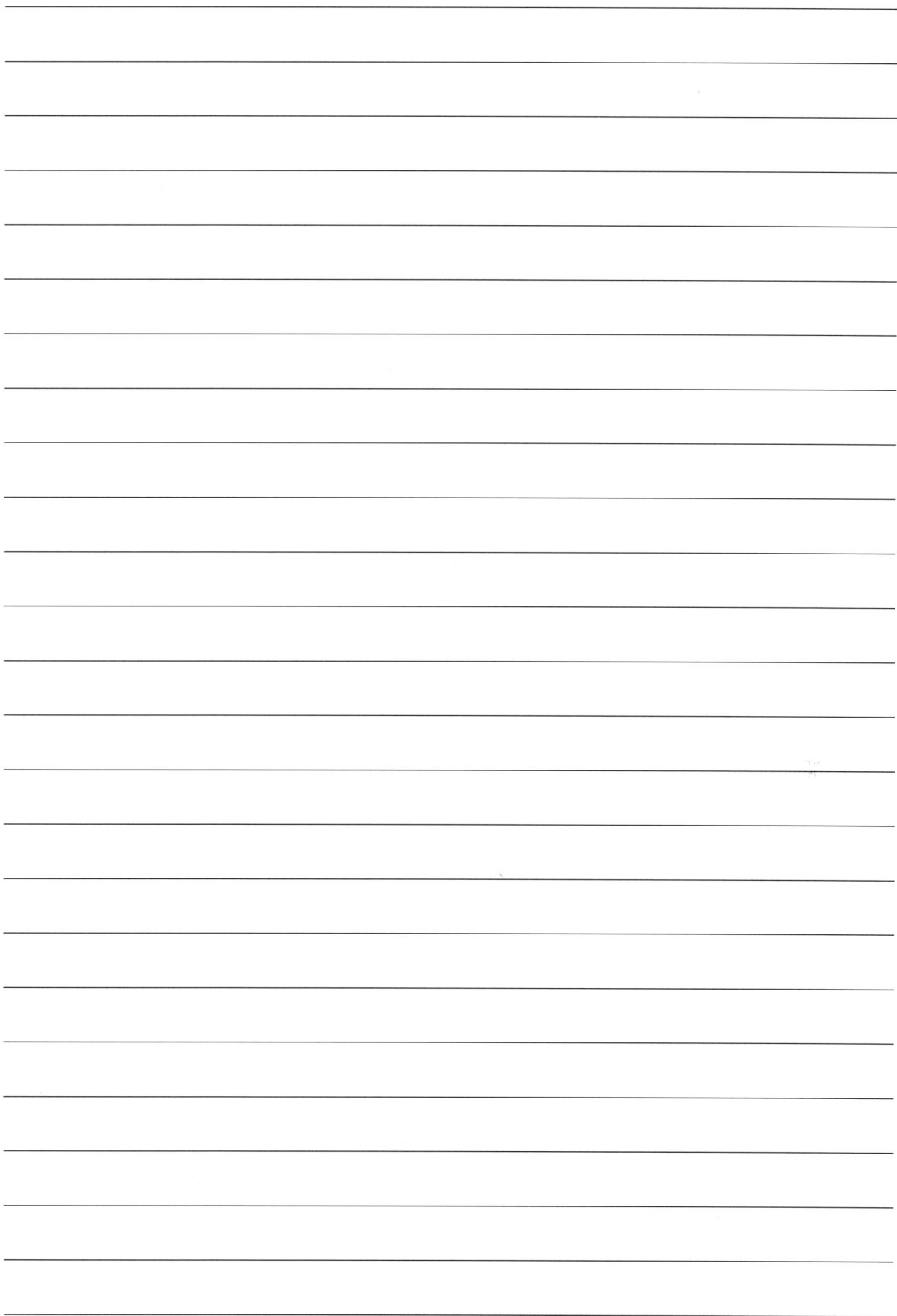

Date:	Anxiety Scale (1-10): AM PM
Today was I compassionate with myself or critical?	Are my thoughts giving me power or taking it away?

Are my thoughts true? *Really true?*

Am I avoiding something that I need to deal with?

Am I forecasting the future?

Am I "catastrophizing"?

Did I experience fear today?	Did it actually come true?
What helps to ease my anxiety?	Did I remember that?
Did I nourish my body and drink enough water?	Did I get fresh air?
How did I move my body today?	Did I try to practice mindfulness and deep breathing?
Did I have "What if's" today?	I am grateful for:

Promise me you'll always remember:
You're braver than you believe, stronger than you seem and smarter than you think.
A.A. Milne

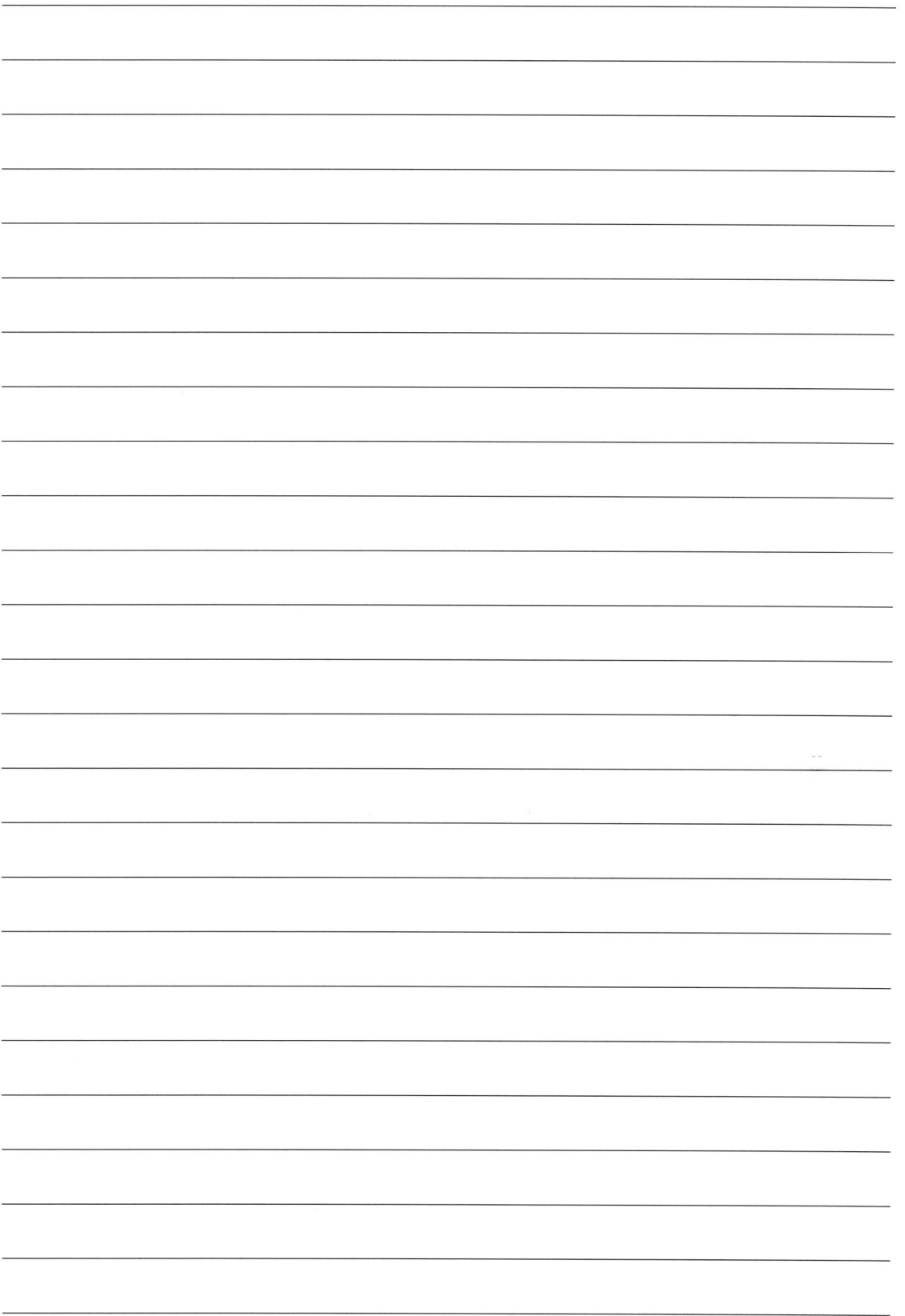

Date:	Anxiety Scale (1-10): AM PM
Today was I compassionate with myself or critical?	Are my thoughts giving me power or taking it away?

Are my thoughts true? *Really true?*

Am I avoiding something that I need to deal with?

Am I forecasting the future?

Am I "catastrophizing"?

Did I experience fear today?	Did it actually come true?
What helps to ease my anxiety?	Did I remember that?
Did I nourish my body and drink enough water?	Did I get fresh air?
How did I move my body today?	Did I try to practice mindfulness and deep breathing?
Did I have "What if's" today?	I am grateful for:

Promise me you'll always remember:
You're braver than you believe, stronger than you seem and smarter than you think.
A.A. Milne

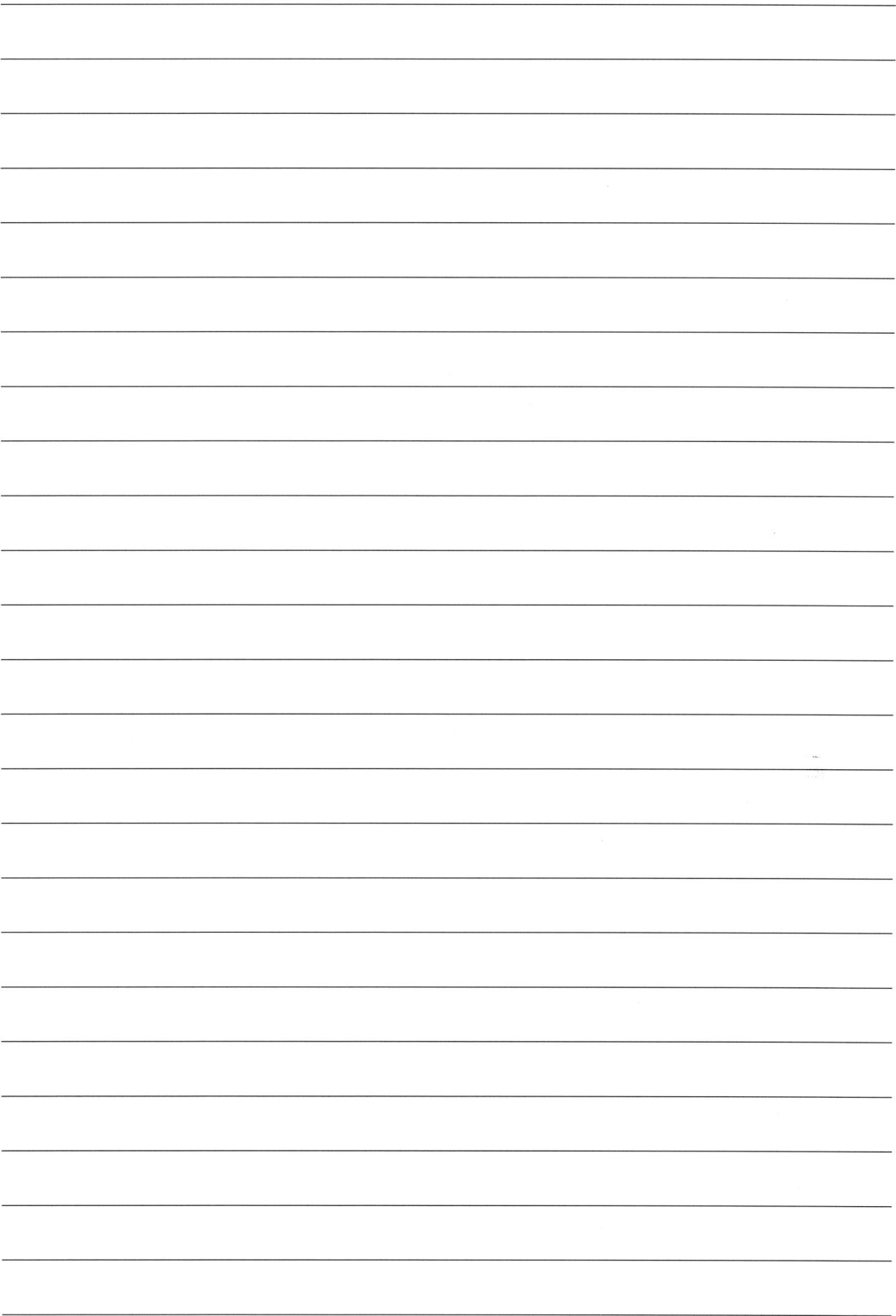

REVIEW OF LAST WEEK

Overall my week was...

Did I have the support I needed?

Did I ask for help when I needed it?

Did I remember my intentions from last week?

Did I spend enough time being unplugged?

I am proud that I....

Notes:

WEEKLY CHECK-IN

My Intention for Next Week:

I would like to:

Experience...

Let go of...

Feel...

Learn to...

Stop...

I want more...	I want less...

Date:	Anxiety Scale (1-10): AM PM
Today was I compassionate with myself or critical?	Are my thoughts giving me power or taking it away?
Are my thoughts true? *Really true?*	
Am I avoiding something that I need to deal with?	
Am I forecasting the future?	
Am I "catastrophizing"?	
Did I experience fear today?	Did it actually come true?
What helps to ease my anxiety?	Did I remember that?
Did I nourish my body and drink enough water?	Did I get fresh air?
How did I move my body today?	Did I try to practice mindfulness and deep breathing?
Did I have "What if's" today?	I am grateful for:

Promise me you'll always remember:
You're braver than you believe, stronger than you seem and smarter than you think.
A.A. Milne

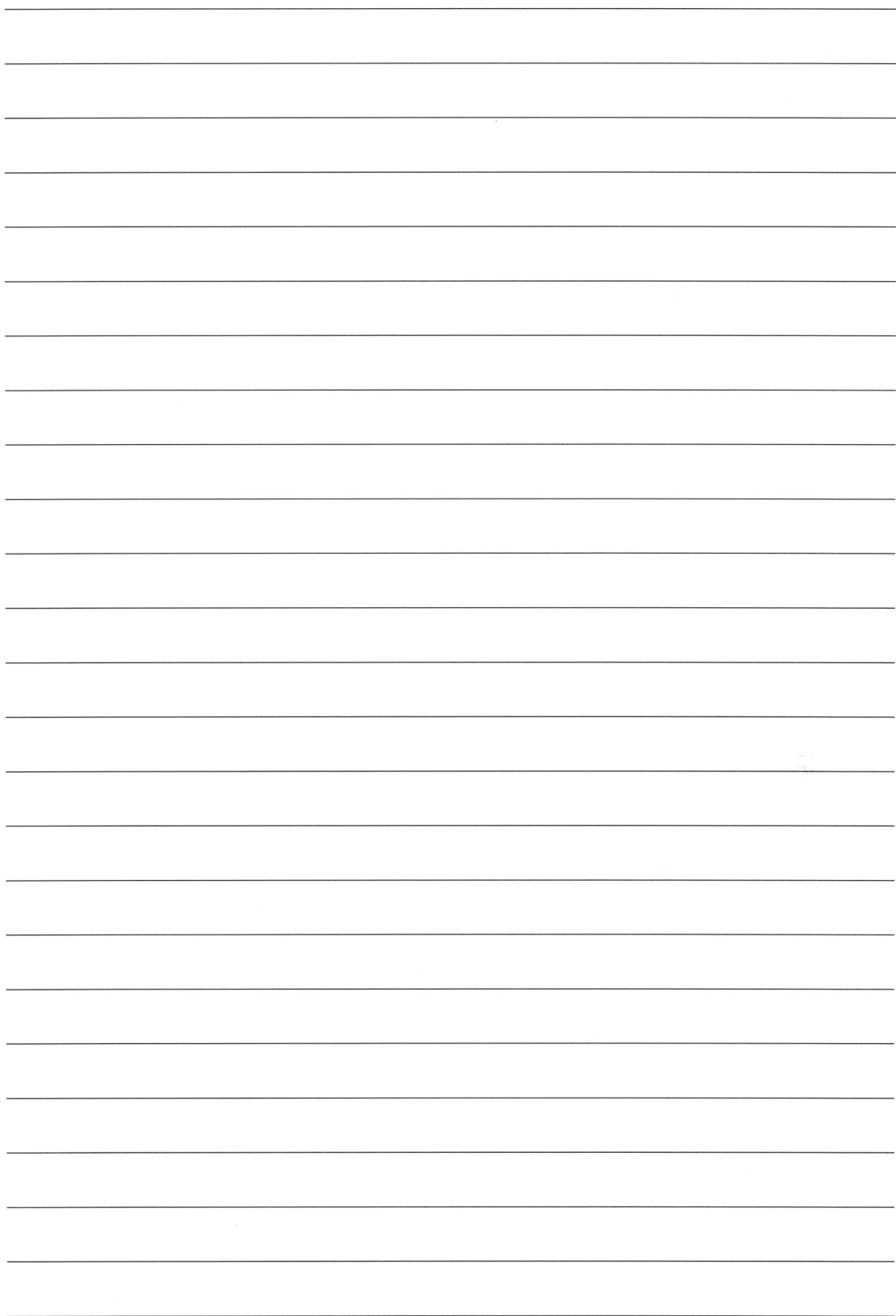

Date:	Anxiety Scale (1-10): AM PM
Today was I compassionate with myself or critical?	Are my thoughts giving me power or taking it away?

Are my thoughts true? *Really true?*

Am I avoiding something that I need to deal with?

Am I forecasting the future?

Am I "catastrophizing"?

Did I experience fear today?	Did it actually come true?
What helps to ease my anxiety?	Did I remember that?
Did I nourish my body and drink enough water?	Did I get fresh air?
How did I move my body today?	Did I try to practice mindfulness and deep breathing?
Did I have "What if's" today?	I am grateful for:

Promise me you'll always remember: You're braver than you believe, stronger than you seem and smarter than you think. *A.A. Milne*

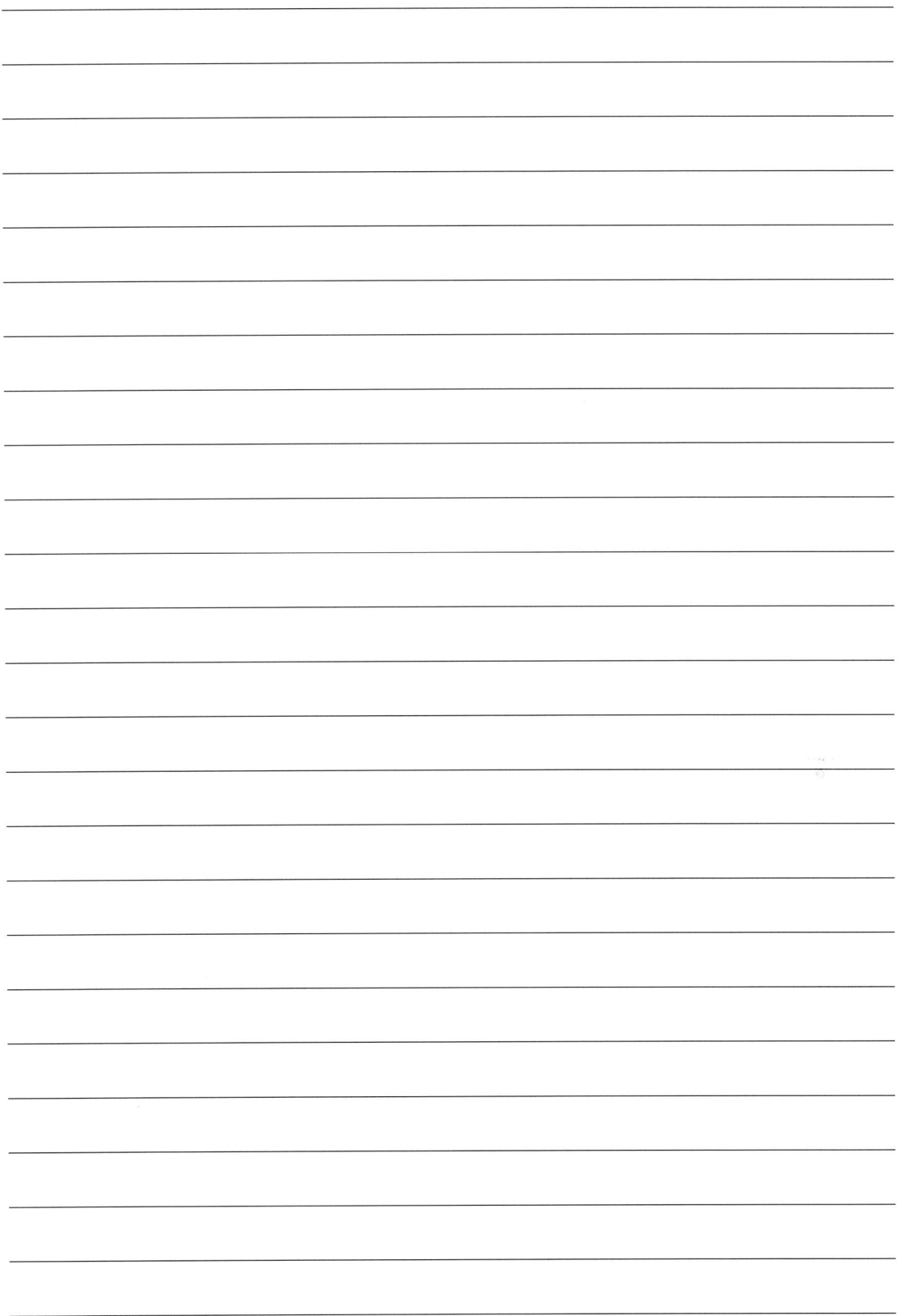

Date:	Anxiety Scale (1-10): AM PM
Today was I compassionate with myself or critical?	Are my thoughts giving me power or taking it away?

Are my thoughts true? *Really true?*

Am I avoiding something that I need to deal with?

Am I forecasting the future?

Am I "catastrophizing"?

Did I experience fear today?	Did it actually come true?
What helps to ease my anxiety?	Did I remember that?
Did I nourish my body and drink enough water?	Did I get fresh air?
How did I move my body today?	Did I try to practice mindfulness and deep breathing?
Did I have "What if's" today?	I am grateful for:

Promise me you'll always remember: You're braver than you believe, stronger than you seem and smarter than you think. *A.A. Milne*

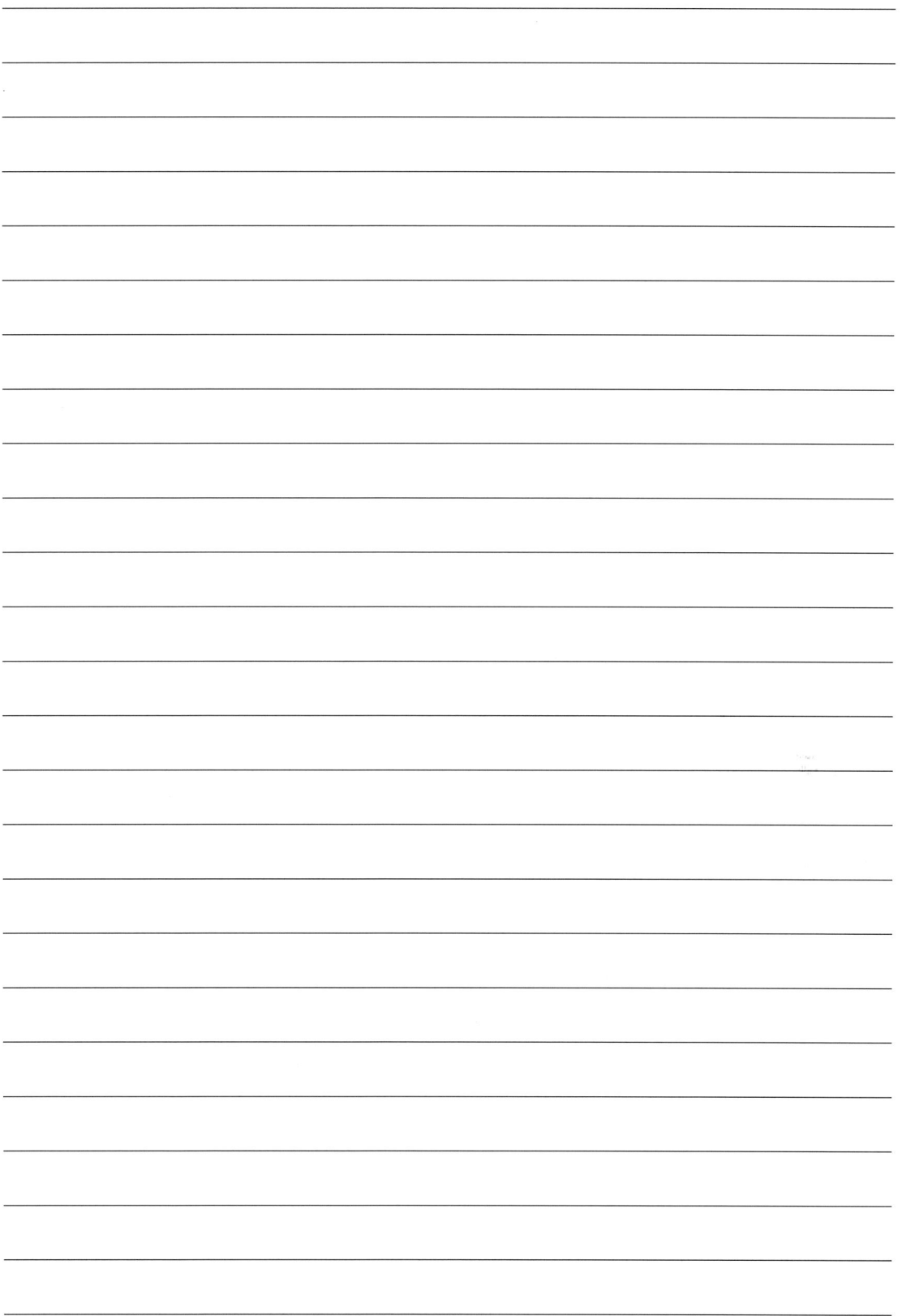

Date:	Anxiety Scale (1-10): AM PM
Today was I compassionate with myself or critical?	Are my thoughts giving me power or taking it away?

Are my thoughts true? *Really true?*

Am I avoiding something that I need to deal with?

Am I forecasting the future?

Am I "catastrophizing"?

Did I experience fear today?	Did it actually come true?
What helps to ease my anxiety?	Did I remember that?
Did I nourish my body and drink enough water?	Did I get fresh air?
How did I move my body today?	Did I try to practice mindfulness and deep breathing?
Did I have "What if's" today?	I am grateful for:

Promise me you'll always remember:
You're braver than you believe, stronger than you seem and smarter than you think.
A.A. Milne

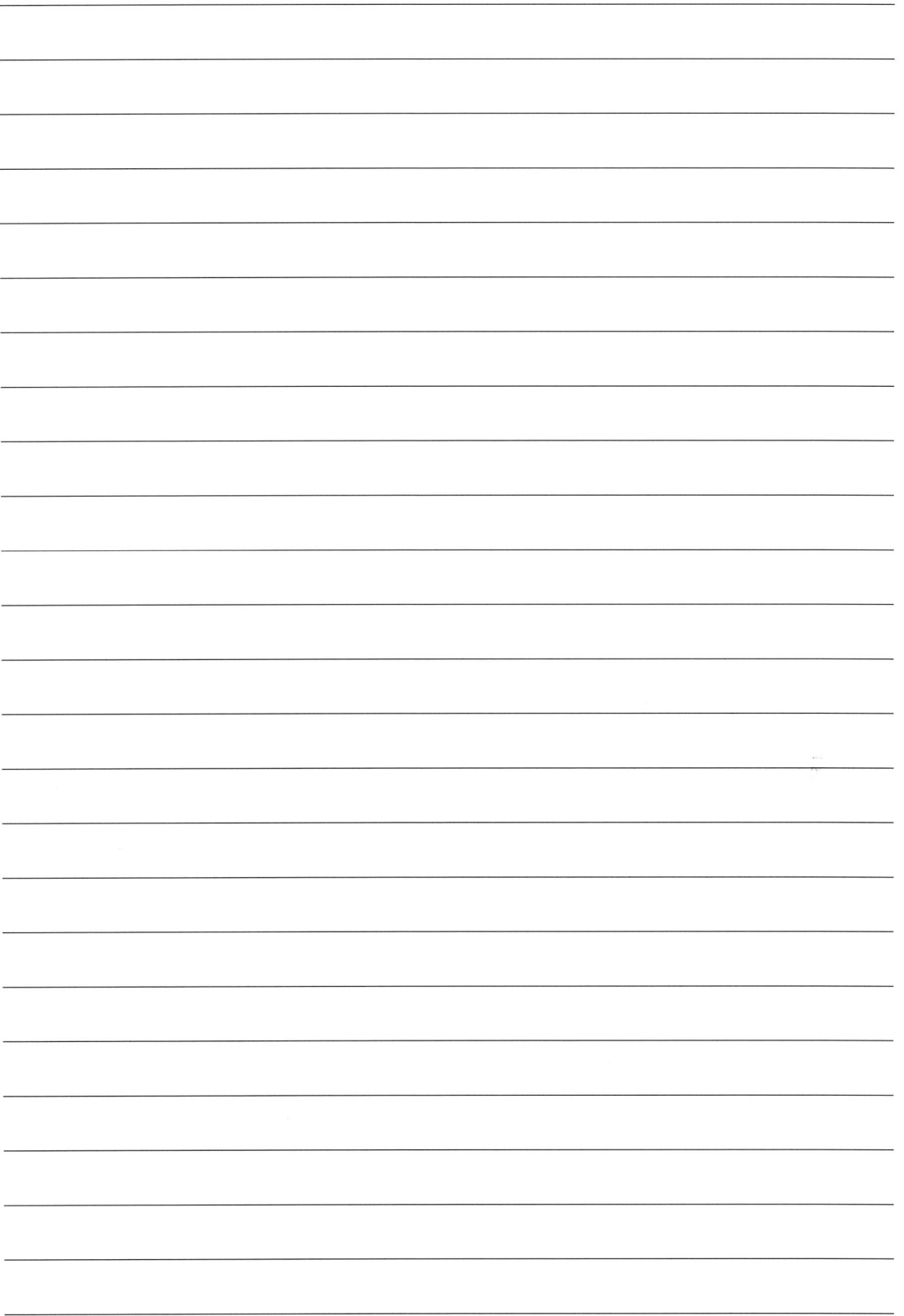

Date:	Anxiety Scale (1-10): AM PM
Today was I compassionate with myself or critical?	Are my thoughts giving me power or taking it away?

Are my thoughts true? *Really true?*
Am I avoiding something that I need to deal with?
Am I forecasting the future?
Am I "catastrophizing"?

Did I experience fear today?	Did it actually come true?
What helps to ease my anxiety?	Did I remember that?
Did I nourish my body and drink enough water?	Did I get fresh air?
How did I move my body today?	Did I try to practice mindfulness and deep breathing?
Did I have "What if's" today?	I am grateful for:

Promise me you'll always remember:
You're braver than you believe, stronger than you seem and smarter than you think.
A.A. Milne

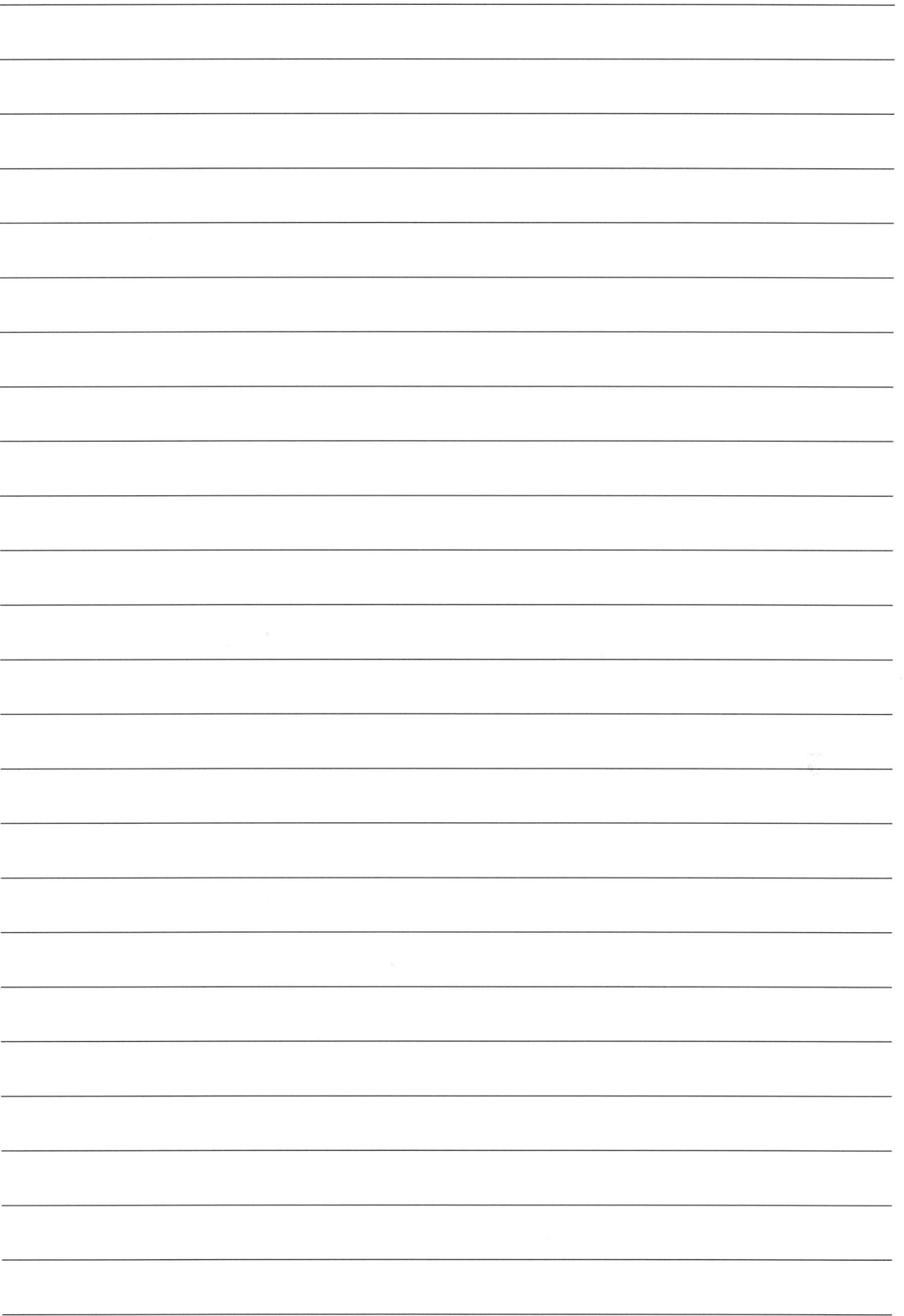

Date:	Anxiety Scale (1-10): AM PM
Today was I compassionate with myself or critical?	Are my thoughts giving me power or taking it away?

Are my thoughts true? *Really true?*

Am I avoiding something that I need to deal with?

Am I forecasting the future?

Am I "catastrophizing"?

Did I experience fear today?	Did it actually come true?

What helps to ease my anxiety?	Did I remember that?

Did I nourish my body and drink enough water?	Did I get fresh air?

How did I move my body today?	Did I try to practice mindfulness and deep breathing?

Did I have "What if's" today?	I am grateful for:

Promise me you'll always remember:
You're braver than you believe, stronger than you seem and smarter than you think.
A.A. Milne

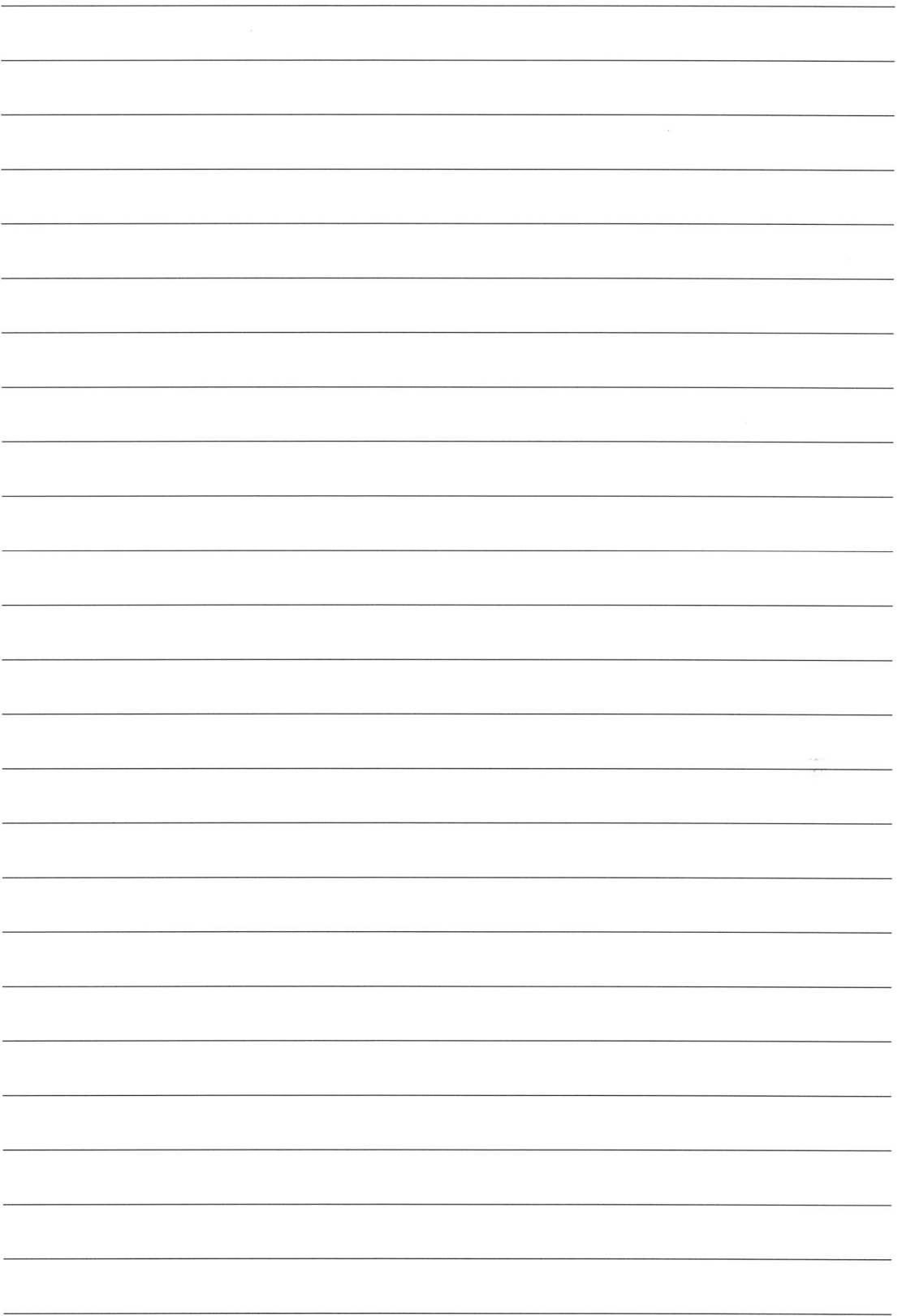

Date:	Anxiety Scale (1-10): AM PM
Today was I compassionate with myself or critical?	Are my thoughts giving me power or taking it away?

Are my thoughts true? *Really true?*

Am I avoiding something that I need to deal with?

Am I forecasting the future?

Am I "catastrophizing"?

Did I experience fear today?	Did it actually come true?
What helps to ease my anxiety?	Did I remember that?
Did I nourish my body and drink enough water?	Did I get fresh air?
How did I move my body today?	Did I try to practice mindfulness and deep breathing?
Did I have "What if's" today?	I am grateful for:

Promise me you'll always remember:
You're braver than you believe, stronger than you seem and smarter than you think.
A.A. Milne

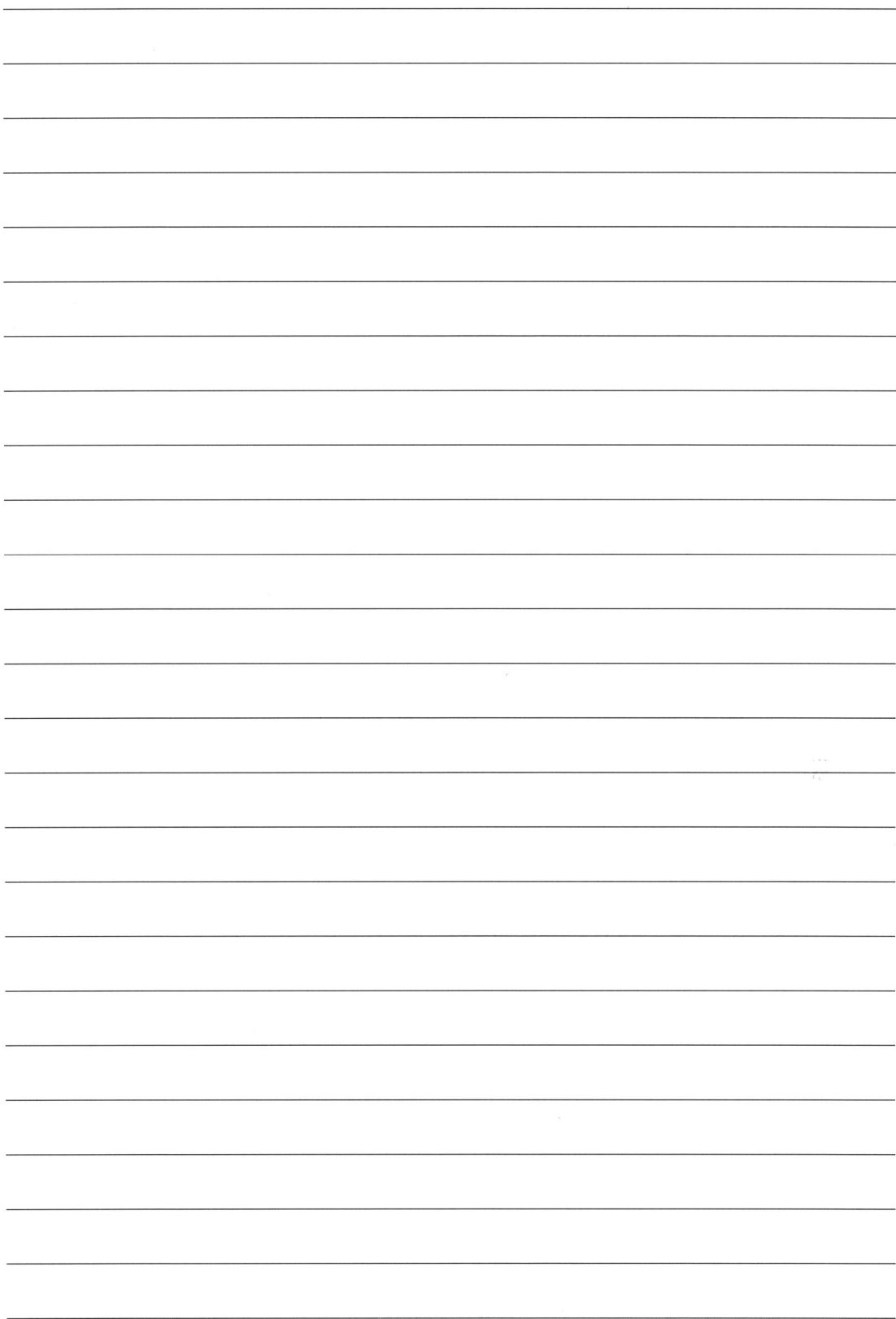

REVIEW OF LAST WEEK

Overall my week was...

Did I have the support I needed?

Did I ask for help when I needed it?

Did I remember my intentions from last week?

Did I spend enough time being unplugged?

I am proud that I....

Notes:

WEEKLY CHECK-IN

My Intention for Next Week:

I would like to:

Experience…

Let go of…

Feel…

Learn to…

Stop…

I want more…	I want less…

Date:	Anxiety Scale (1-10): AM PM
Today was I compassionate with myself or critical?	Are my thoughts giving me power or taking it away?

Are my thoughts true? *Really true?*

Am I avoiding something that I need to deal with?

Am I forecasting the future?

Am I "catastrophizing"?

Did I experience fear today?	Did it actually come true?
What helps to ease my anxiety?	Did I remember that?
Did I nourish my body and drink enough water?	Did I get fresh air?
How did I move my body today?	Did I try to practice mindfulness and deep breathing?
Did I have "What if's" today?	I am grateful for:

Promise me you'll always remember:
You're braver than you believe, stronger than you seem and smarter than you think.
A.A. Milne

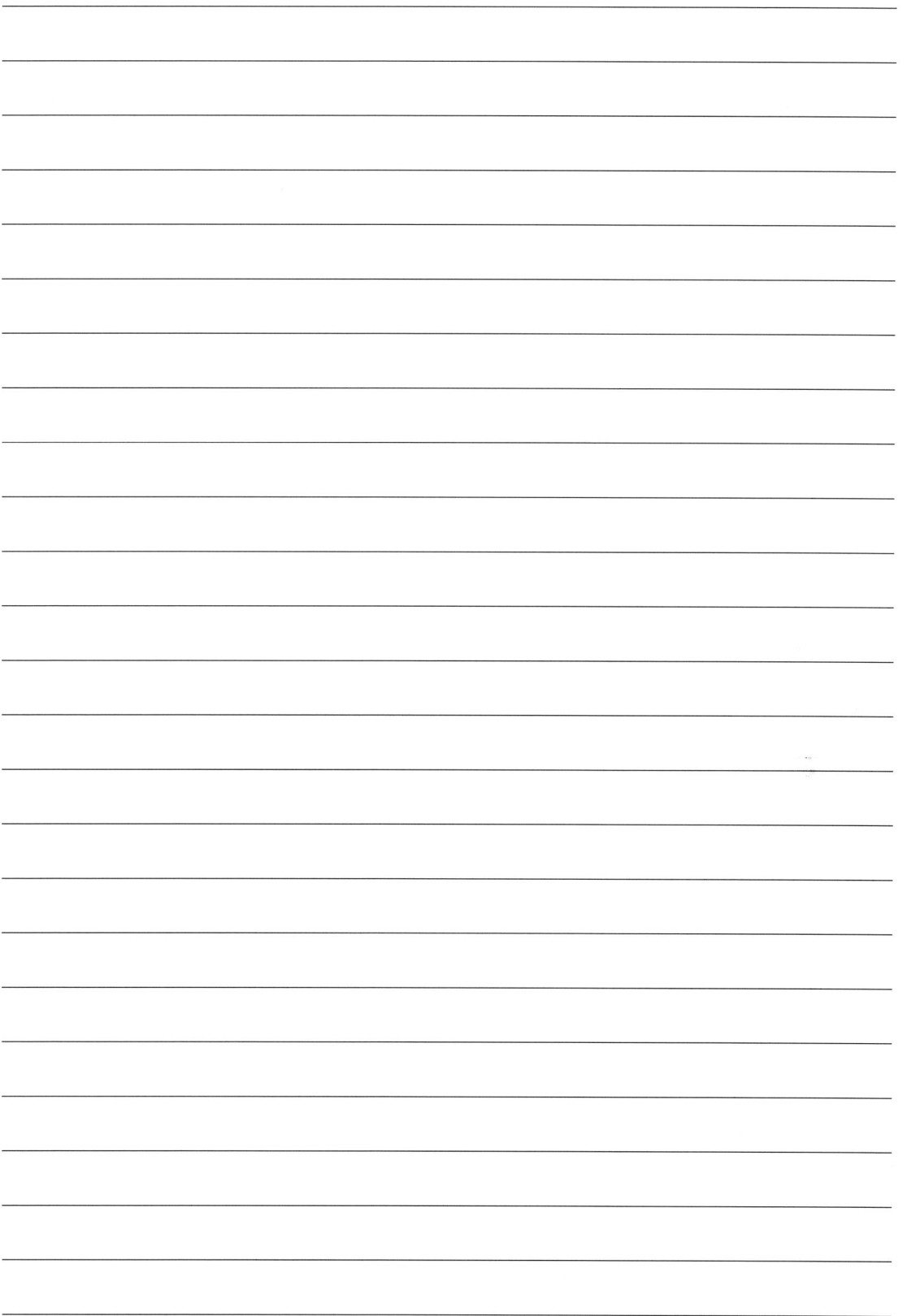

Date:	Anxiety Scale (1-10): AM PM
Today was I compassionate with myself or critical?	Are my thoughts giving me power or taking it away?

Are my thoughts true? *Really true?*

Am I avoiding something that I need to deal with?

Am I forecasting the future?

Am I "catastrophizing"?

Did I experience fear today?	Did it actually come true?
What helps to ease my anxiety?	Did I remember that?
Did I nourish my body and drink enough water?	Did I get fresh air?
How did I move my body today?	Did I try to practice mindfulness and deep breathing?
Did I have "What if's" today?	I am grateful for:

Promise me you'll always remember:
You're braver than you believe, stronger than you seem and smarter than you think.
A.A. Milne

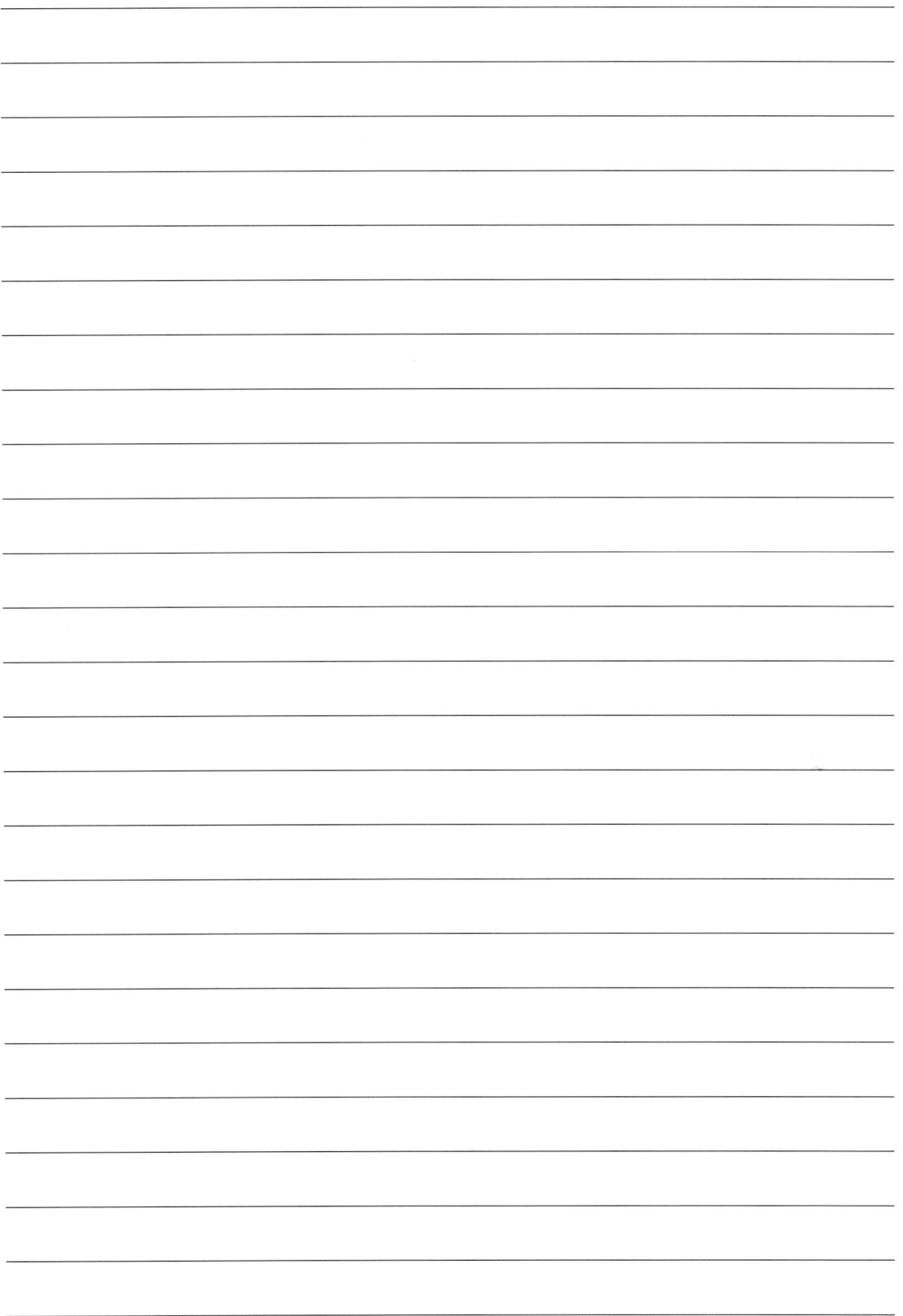

Date:	Anxiety Scale (1-10): AM PM
Today was I compassionate with myself or critical?	Are my thoughts giving me power or taking it away?

Are my thoughts true? *Really true?*

Am I avoiding something that I need to deal with?

Am I forecasting the future?

Am I "catastrophizing"?

Did I experience fear today?	Did it actually come true?
What helps to ease my anxiety?	Did I remember that?
Did I nourish my body and drink enough water?	Did I get fresh air?
How did I move my body today?	Did I try to practice mindfulness and deep breathing?
Did I have "What if's" today?	I am grateful for:

Promise me you'll always remember:
You're braver than you believe, stronger than you seem and smarter than you think.
A.A. Milne

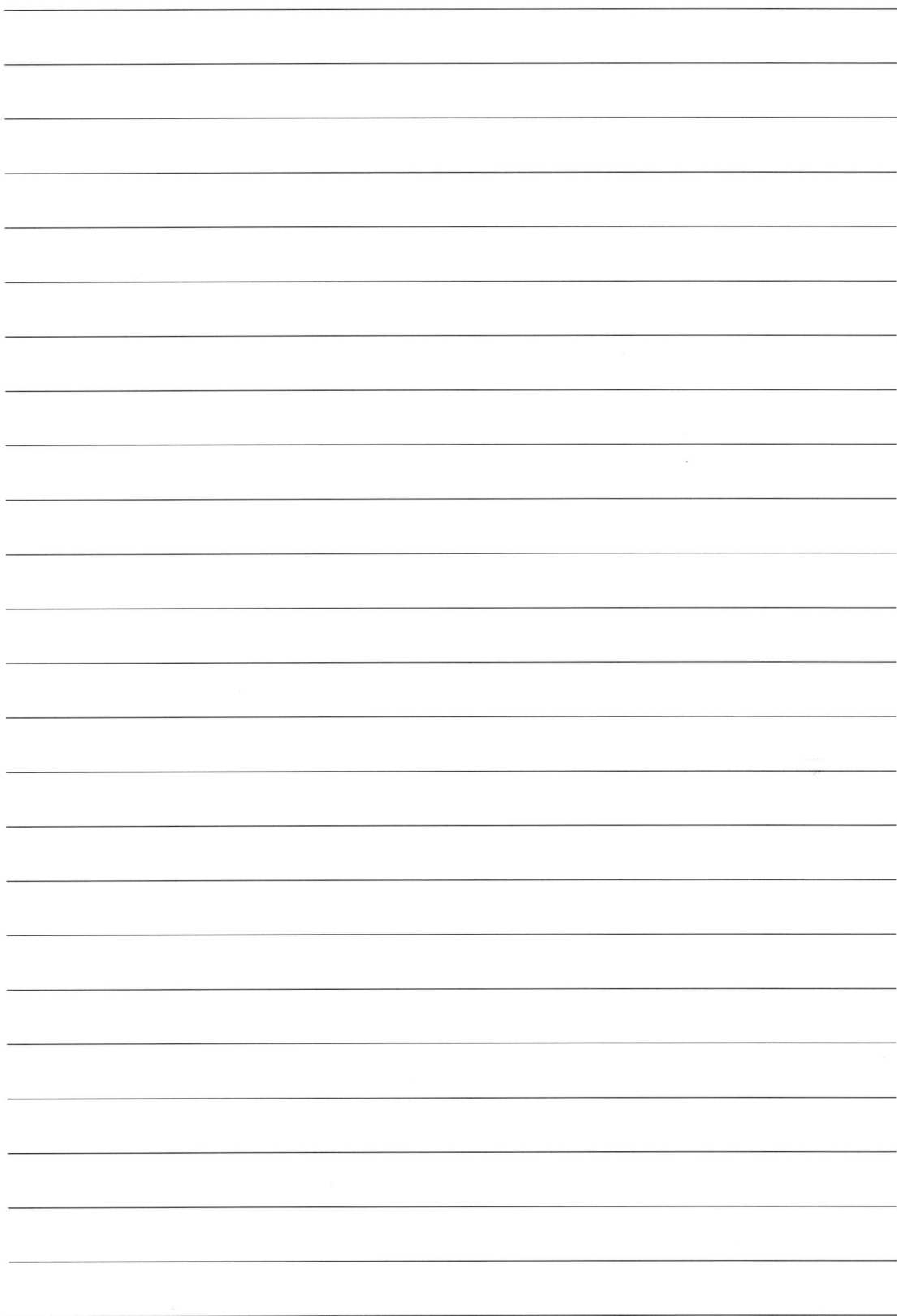

Date:	Anxiety Scale (1-10): AM PM
Today was I compassionate with myself or critical?	Are my thoughts giving me power or taking it away?

Are my thoughts true? *Really true?*

Am I avoiding something that I need to deal with?

Am I forecasting the future?

Am I "catastrophizing"?

Did I experience fear today?	Did it actually come true?
What helps to ease my anxiety?	Did I remember that?
Did I nourish my body and drink enough water?	Did I get fresh air?
How did I move my body today?	Did I try to practice mindfulness and deep breathing?
Did I have "What if's" today?	I am grateful for:

Promise me you'll always remember:
You're braver than you believe, stronger than you seem and smarter than you think.
A.A. Milne

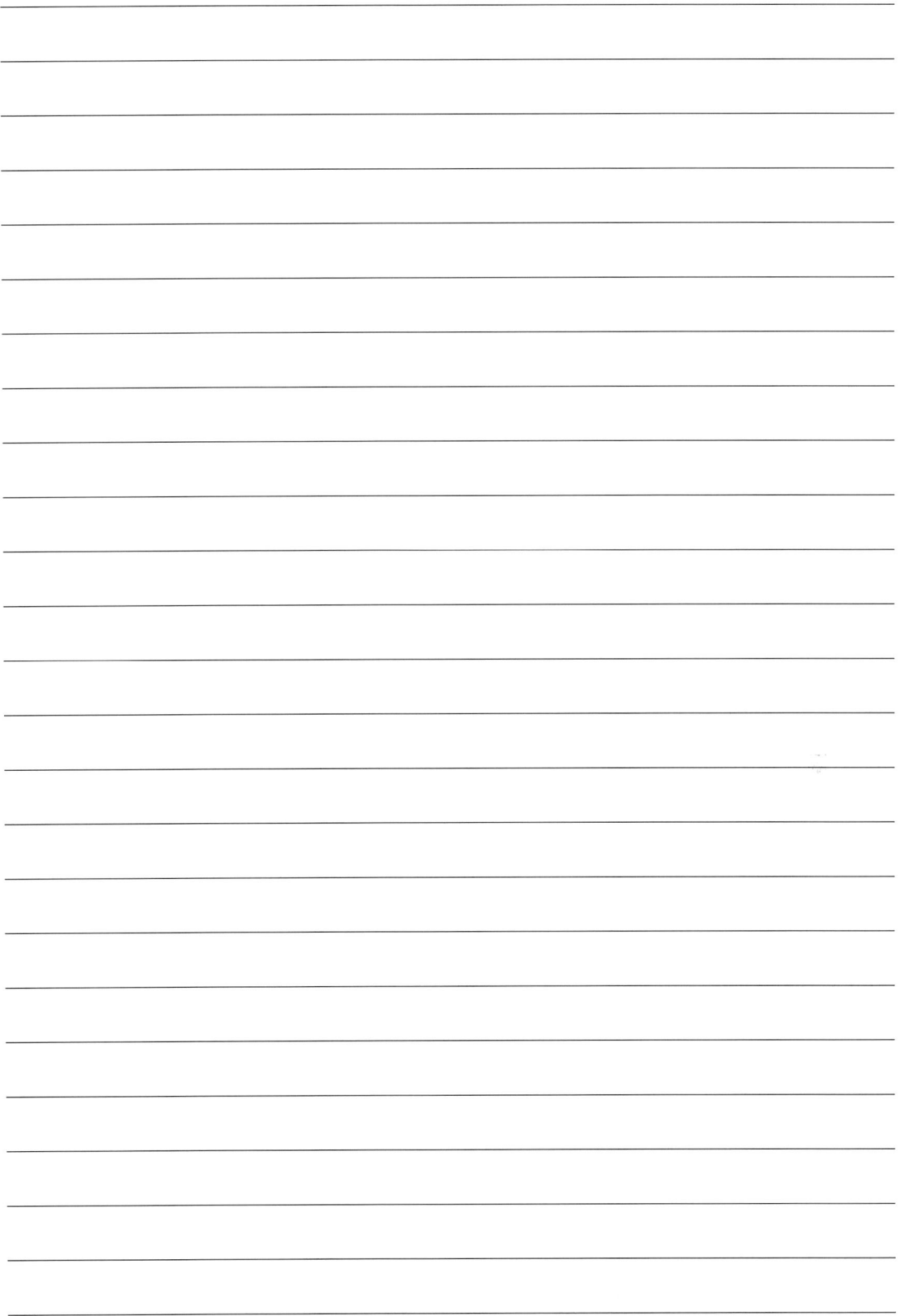

| Date: | Anxiety Scale (1-10): |
	AM PM
Today was I compassionate with myself or critical?	Are my thoughts giving me power or taking it away?

Are my thoughts true? *Really true?*

Am I avoiding something that I need to deal with?

Am I forecasting the future?

Am I "catastrophizing"?

Did I experience fear today?	Did it actually come true?
What helps to ease my anxiety?	Did I remember that?
Did I nourish my body and drink enough water?	Did I get fresh air?
How did I move my body today?	Did I try to practice mindfulness and deep breathing?
Did I have "What if's" today?	I am grateful for:

Promise me you'll always remember:
You're braver than you believe, stronger than you seem and smarter than you think.
A.A. Milne

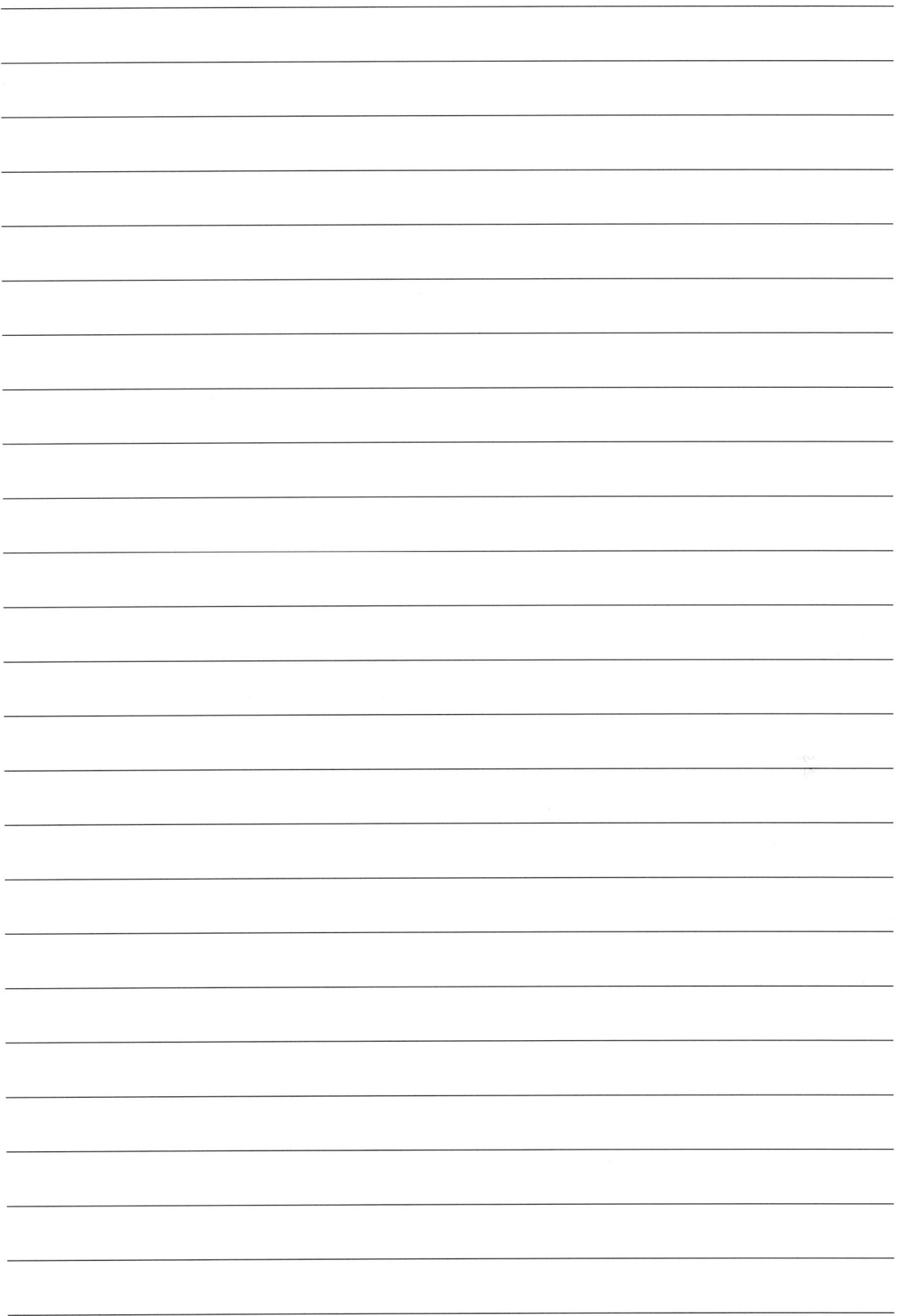

Date:	Anxiety Scale (1-10): AM PM
Today was I compassionate with myself or critical?	Are my thoughts giving me power or taking it away?

Are my thoughts true? *Really true?*

Am I avoiding something that I need to deal with?

Am I forecasting the future?

Am I "catastrophizing"?

Did I experience fear today?	Did it actually come true?
What helps to ease my anxiety?	Did I remember that?
Did I nourish my body and drink enough water?	Did I get fresh air?
How did I move my body today?	Did I try to practice mindfulness and deep breathing?
Did I have "What if's" today?	I am grateful for:

Promise me you'll always remember:
You're braver than you believe, stronger than you seem and smarter than you think.
A.A. Milne

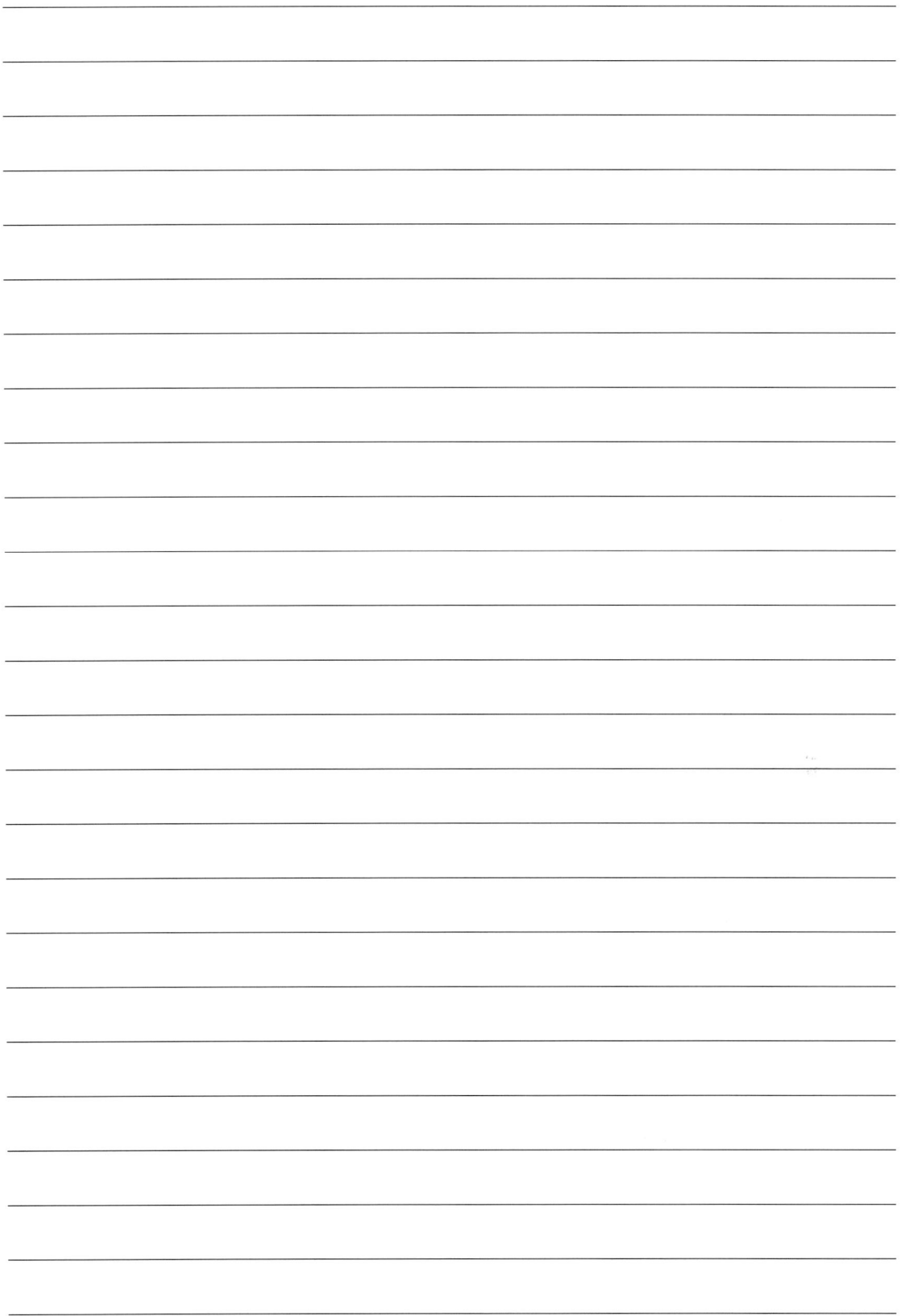

| Date: | Anxiety Scale (1-10): |
| | AM   PM |

| Today was I compassionate with myself or critical? | Are my thoughts giving me power or taking it away? |

Are my thoughts true? *Really true?*

Am I avoiding something that I need to deal with?

Am I forecasting the future?

Am I "catastrophizing"?

| Did I experience fear today? | Did it actually come true? |

| What helps to ease my anxiety? | Did I remember that? |

| Did I nourish my body and drink enough water? | Did I get fresh air? |

| How did I move my body today? | Did I try to practice mindfulness and deep breathing? |

| Did I have "What if's" today? | I am grateful for: |

Promise me you'll always remember:
You're braver than you believe, stronger than you seem and smarter than you think.
A.A. Milne

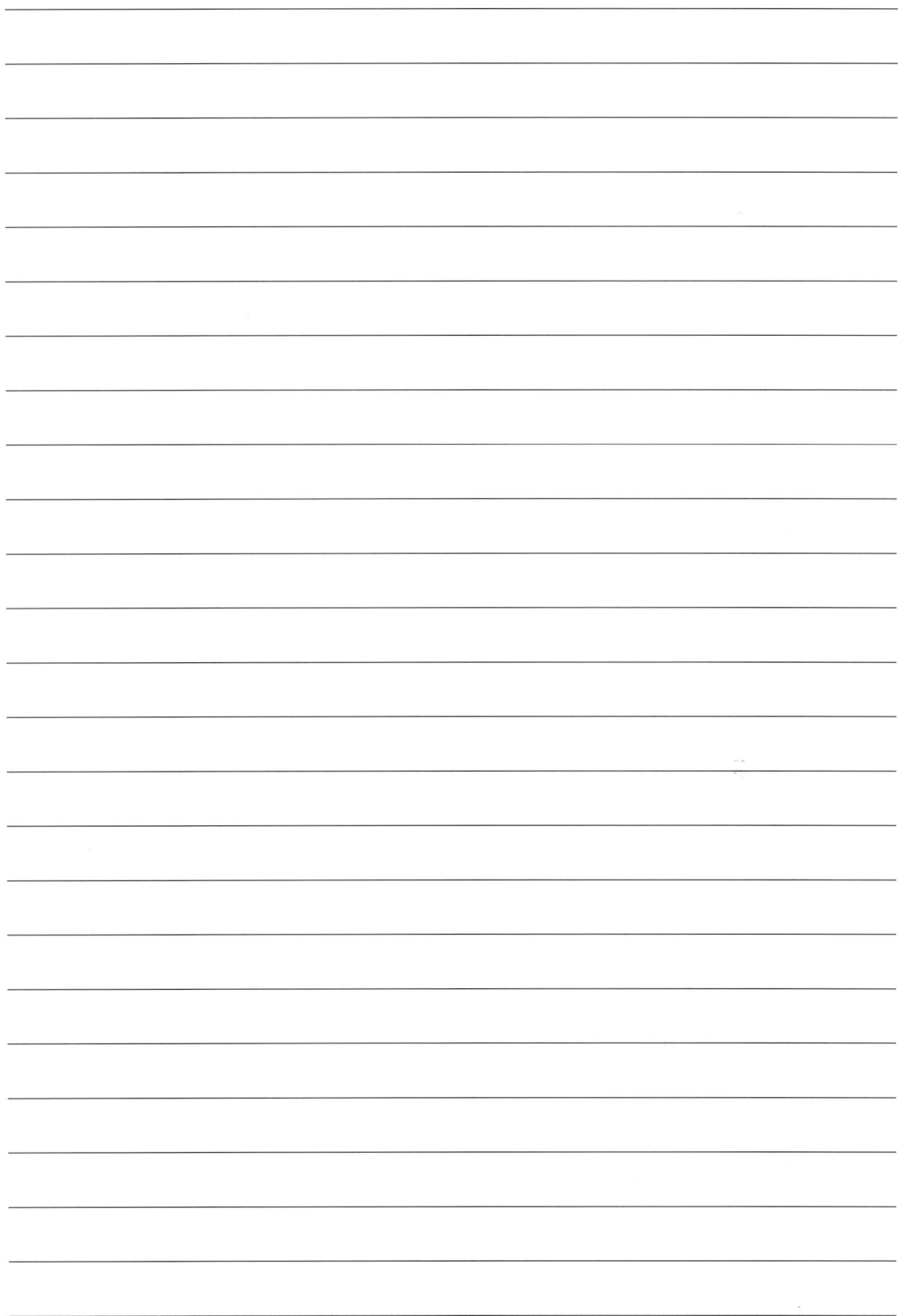

REVIEW OF LAST WEEK

Overall my week was...

Did I have the support I needed?

Did I ask for help when I needed it?

Did I remember my intentions from last week?

Did I spend enough time being unplugged?

I am proud that I....

Notes:

WEEKLY CHECK-IN

My Intention for Next Week:

I would like to:

Experience...

Let go of...

Feel...

Learn to...

Stop...

I want more...	I want less...

Made in the USA
Columbia, SC
09 October 2017

ISBN 9781977849922

90000 >

9 781977 849922